Stummick, Hardbody and Me

A compilation of tall tales and old newspaper columns

about the great outdoors and not-so-great indoors

by

Seabury Blair Jr.

authorHOUSE™

1663 LIBERTY DRIVE, SUITE 200
BLOOMINGTON, INDIANA 47403
(800) 839-8640
WWW.AUTHORHOUSE.COM

First published by AuthorHouse 10/20/05

ISBN: 1-4208-7620-1 (sc)

Library of Congress Control Number: 2005907511

Printed in the United States of America
Bloomington, Indiana

This book is printed on acid-free paper.

Illustrations by: Joe Lee

Cover Design by: April Mostek

Book Design by: Sarah Lauck

Design Consultant: Jenn Handy

CONTENTS

ACKNOWLEDGMENTS

Thanks to my wife, Marlene, for her love, support, and understanding in the face of such withering written abuse as could be mustered on these pages. Thanks to Mike Phillips and Gussie Schaeffer for their belief, beyond reason, that I might indeed learn to write something besides my name, and to the editors and publishers at *The Kitsap Sun* who followed. I am most grateful for the good friends who furnished the inspiration for the tales herein: Mike Archbold, Little Scribe; Jim Drannan, the Gnarly Dude; Dave Holman, Lothario Mudmire; Ron C. Judd, Wimpfoot; John McCurdy, Grizzly Hemingway; Ron Ramey, the Scotch Hippie; and, last only alphabetically, Dan Weaver, the Big Scribe. Thanks, too, to Skip the Scott and Sharon the Strong, Skip and Sharon McKenzie. Finally, the author wishes to thank all the planners, consultants, and emergency services coordinators for all the good work they do, whatever that may be.

INTRODUCTION

It is my abiding hope that at least one of the twenty people who sees this book will find something in its pages about which to chuckle—perhaps even laugh. You may wonder: How do I know twenty people will see this book? Because I had to promise the publisher I would buy twenty books before they agreed to print it, and I have no intention of keeping these tomes around my house any longer than is absolutely necessary.

So my plan is to give these volumes to twenty of my friends, pleading that they read at least one of the pages before they commit their gift to the shelf or, more likely, the shredder. I expect to bribe with real money at least five of these individuals, since they might more accurately be described as acquaintances rather than friends. I'm guessing the remaining fifteen may suggest I consider them acquaintances as well, especially if they read anything herein.

First, a bit of history: In what I am certain was a lapse in sanity, Mike Phillips, the former editor and publisher of *The Sun* (the daily newspaper in Bremerton, Washington, where I avoided work for three decades) decided more than fifteen years ago that I could write a weekly column for a new Sunday section of the paper that dealt with travel and outdoor recreation. I fully expected that at any moment, Phillips would come to his senses and dump me faster than you can spell r-e-c-y-c-l-e. I believe to this day he must have been overmedicated—or that something clouded his normal brilliance—for about eight years, because I survived until 1999. If I recall correctly, it was that year the good people at Scripps Howard promoted Mike to a corporate position and he left town. Certain that the new editor or publisher would have far better taste or be more sane than Phillips, I retired to write three guidebooks, which—I am proud to say—have only caused two people (that I know of) to become hopelessly lost.

But before Phillips left, I convinced him to let me write another weekly column for *The Sun*. It was supposed to be funny, and I took it as a sign of Mike's deteriorated mental condition that he actually laughed at the sample column I showed him. The subject was the difference between speed humps and speed bumps, so you can make your own judgment about his psychosocial state. Though I am quite convinced that one had little to do with the other, he got out of town shortly thereafter and the new editors and publishers were stuck with me for more than five years. They weathered the storm quite well; those who truly suffered were the loyal readers who every Friday thought I could not possibly go another week without writing something funny and foolishly gave me another chance. I hereby dedicate this book to them.

On the following pages, you'll find some of the columns I wrote during the past fifteen years. Many, but not all, are based loosely upon events that actually occurred, but may contain slight exaggerations, perhaps downright lies. Most of the characters who populate these pages are modeled after real people; that they actually said or did any of the things I ascribe to them is a matter of how you define such words as "factual" and "accurate." I've made every effort to update and revise the columns so they might be more relevant and timely, but basically you'll be reading the same stuff you may have read back in 1994 or 2002. So if any of the following sounds familiar, I apologize. Please forgive me and move on to the next tall tale. Still, I'm staking my twenty books on the premise that I gave few readers—even then—any cause to remember what I wrote from one week to the next.

Seabury Blair Jr.
Lake Slimeington

I.   WORTHLESS ADVICE

THE NWRD IF THOT THEF FINGH

ANTHRAX! There, I said it. Anthrax, anthrax, anthrax.

I said it three more times. Did you know that the more times you repeat a word, the less frightening the word becomes?

It's true. I learned that in my Basic Communications class at the University of Confusion (Pysht, Washington campus). That was back when Washington was still a territory. The professor of my Basic Communications class stood in front of the group and said, "The word is not the thing. The word will not hurt you."

Actually, that is not what the professor said. The professor of my Basic Communications class had a speech impediment. He said, "Thef nwrd if thot thef fingh. Thef nwrd fwl thot fwrt foo."

Nobody could understand my Basic Communications professor. So it was up to Vinnie, his teaching assistant, to translate all of the professor's lectures. It was during one of those lectures that I learned the more times you repeat a word, the less threatening it becomes.

Try it with me: Anthrax. Anthrax. Anthrax. Anthrax. Anthrax. Anthrax. Anthrax. And finally, anthrax.

See? It really works. I'll bet you'll open twice as much junk mail as you opened back in the days when those bad guys were packing anthrax into every envelope in your mailbox.

I remember that B.B. Hardbody brought in the mail and the only thing addressed to me was a bulky envelope from Florida.

"You'd better wash your hands," I told her. "Better yet, maybe you'd better strip nekid and let me hose you down."

As is her custom, Hardbody just laughed at my pathetic attempt to get her clothes off. I figured something as serious as anthrax might do the trick. I took the letter and immediately applied all of the techniques I learned in CBR Warfare Training when I was in the Army, shortly after Washington became a state. CBR is the abbreviation for "Chemical-Biological-Radiological." I placed the letter in a plastic bag. Then I opened it carefully and slowly, so that the suspicious white powder inside would not spill out.

Of course there was no suspicious white powder. It was a solicitation from the Florida Citrus Fruit-of-the-Month Club. Still, you can't be too careful, so I recommend that even in these more enlightened times today, you practice the following tips with any suspicious junk mail:

—Never open an e-mail containing white powder; or, for that matter, powder of any color.

—Do not open any letters bearing the return address: "The Taliban, Afghanistan," or "Osama Bin Laden," especially if they are written in Arabic.

—If you receive a free sample of baby powder or powdered sugar in the mail, the prudent course would be to avoid sticking either envelope up your nose.

—Don't open any mail addressed to "Occupant," unless of course that is your name. This advice has nothing to do with anthrax, but a whole lot to do with the incredible amount of junk sent through the U.S. mail every day.

—Finally, always keep in mind that it is the fingh that is dangerous, not the nwrd.

BE AFRAID. BE VERY AFRAID

Like all good Americans, I've been on the alert for suspicious persons who might be terrorists. And perhaps like many of you, I'm a little worried about being able to spot a terrorist.

Sure, I suppose I wouldn't have problems identifying a terrorist if he asked me to check out his truck full of C4 explosives or wanted me to admire his Uzi. But if you discount race, religion, or ethnic background— which you should by all means—a terrorist could be just about anyone.

I mentioned my concern to B.B. Hardbody the other day. "I have issues," I said, "about being terrorized."

Hardbody's reply was terse.

"You needn't worry. You are a terror."

I suppose she's right about not worrying. I mean, if you want to kill a bunch of people, you are not likely to attack the places you will find me. Hardly a soul frequents my favorite pub, Cheap Beer and Stale Popcorn, anymore.

And Hardbody says it would be the height of egotism and conceit for me to think that a terrorist would go after me in the backcountry. Collateral damage might amount to an elk and maybe a hibernating marmot or two.

So I've been thinking about ways to overcome my rampant paranoia. It is important to come up with a constructive means of identifying actual suspicious behavior, the kind of stuff that would not cause a Department of Homeland Security official to convulse on the floor with laughter for two weeks. I think I've come up with a few helpful distinctions. Consider for yourself:

—If you see a woman wearing dark glasses wheeling a baby carriage past the front gate of a nuclear submarine base, and she keeps glancing up the road as if she were expecting someone, there is little cause for suspicion. It is likely that she is waiting for a bus, not for a truckload of C4.

If, on the other hand, you see a woman wearing dark glasses wheeling a baby carriage past the front gate of a nuclear submarine base, and the baby in the carriage has a metal body with foreign writing that translates to "EXPLOSIVE" or "RADIOACTIVE," you may be justified in your suspicion.

—Don't be alarmed if anyone carries a Swiss Army knife or shows off the number of blades on it. I myself carry a Swiss Army knife with sixty-two blades, including a miniature chainsaw and an emergency tent.

Be suspicious of anyone carrying a Swiss Army

knife that has as one of its blades a canister labeled "Terrorist-Grade Plutonium," or if the knife is ticking loudly.

—Far too many people these days can be seen driving autos while talking on their cell phones. There is little reason to be suspicious of these people, although many of you would agree they are indeed a danger to others.

If, on the other hand, you see someone talking on a cell phone while waving a scimitar and pointing an Uzi at the driver, you might be justified in notifying the authorities. I guess what I am saying is: Keep your wits about you and I'll be certain to keep at least half of mine.

PUBLIC MISINFORMATION

A couple of years ago, keyless remote devices on brand-new automobiles in our neck of the woods stopped working. **AND THE NAVY CLAIMED IT KNEW NOTHING ABOUT IT.**

You could be locked out of your brand-new car and if you didn't have a real key, you'd be out of luck. You spent a couple of hundred bucks or more on some fancy hunk of hardware that just stopped working.

Everybody but the Navy figured the arrival of that big warship had something to do with it. It seems the keyless entry systems stopped working about the time the ship pulled into port. I figure some poor enlisted man forgot to turn off the electronic device that fries other electronic devices. At least, that is the theory the Navy said it knew nothing about. And that is the part of the story that is funny to me: trying to imagine what other explanations there might be.

I served our great country as a Public Information Specialist in the U.S. Army. It was my job to make up other explanations for things the Army did, but did not want to confirm. For example—and this is purely a hypothetical case—when a helicopter flew into the side of a mountain in the fog because some poor enlisted man forgot to turn on the radar, a Public Information Specialist like me sprang into duty. He or she made up other explanations about why the helicopter flew into the side of a mountain, because the Army did not want to confirm that some poor enlisted man forgot to turn on the radar.

These explanations were then passed on to the Public Information Officer, who would not confirm anything. But the officer did offer our other explanations.

I have some experience at making up other explanations, as I say. So here's a few the Navy can use the next time keyless entry systems stop working:

1. Large flocks of seagulls, which have electromagnetic sensors in their heads just behind their beaks, can generate powerful electronic fields capable of disrupting keyless entry systems. The biggest flock of seagulls to gather in recent history followed the warship into port.

2. Certain types of 1950s Virginia fiddle music played badly on period instruments not only causes widespread electronic disruption, but major mental problems including disorientation and stupidity. It is

a little-known fact that the Roanoke Ramblers Revival was held the very weekend those keyless things stopped working.

3. Virtually all of our electronic reserves are being used as millions try to send buy and sell orders on the Internet. This causes massive disruption of the keyless entry electronic continuum.

4. Sunspots, which, as everyone knows, cause interference with radio reception and magnificent displays of the Northern Lights, don't usually affect keyless entry systems. However, when sunspots occur in conjunction with the vernal equinox, two phenomena are evident:

a) Keyless entries stop working.

b) The Navy knows nothing about it.

MY HEART GOES BANGADA

Have you ever wakened in the middle of the night to feel your heart beating like this: bangada-bangada-bing-bing? I have, and it nearly frightened me to death.

Your heart is supposed to sound like Patrick Swayze describes it to Jennifer Gray in my most favorite movie of all time, *Dirty Dancing*. He's trying to teach her the pachinga, or the panko, or whatever fancy dance it is, and he tells Jennifer, "You got to feel it, just like a heartbeat."

Then he takes her hand and holds it on his heart and says, "Ka-chunk, ka-chunk." That's the way your heart is supposed to sound.

But mine was beating like this: bangada-bangada-bing-bing. Luckily, it did not frighten me all the way to death, or I would not have been able to call Doc Leo the next morning. I figured all I needed to do was tell Doc Leo how my heart was beating and he would tell me what was wrong and give me a prescription to make me all better. I figured it would be the same as telling your auto mechanic that your car sounded like this: bumpada-bumpada-snick-POP! Then your auto mechanic would say, "Oh, that's nothing serious. It's just the breather mafinade in the calgatator that needs a shot of WD-40." And he would shoot some stuff in there and make your car all better.

But Doc Leo decided I should get something called a "treadmill test." They put you on this treadmill and wire you up to a big calgatator with a TV screen that shows what your heart is doing while you run to Denver and back. Donna, the woman who wired me, decided I had too much hair on my chest where they stick the wires to the calgatator. She had to shave little spots on my chest. I told her that when you have as little hair as I do on my head, the stuff on the rest of my body is sacred. But it didn't seem to do any good.

As soon as I was wired up, Donna and Doc Leo showed me the little spikes on the TV screen that indicated my heart was going bumpada-bumpada-bing-bing. Then they made me run to Denver and back and my heart was beating the same way, only in capital letters with three or four exclamation points at the end.

I think Doc Leo would have liked me to run to Chicago and back, too, but the room was awash in my sweat and smelled like the locker room at the Y around

8 a.m. I was perspiring so profusely I shorted out the calgatator, so the Denver run had to suffice. I figured that armed with the evidence from the calgatator, Doc Leo would prescribe something that would make my heart go ka-chunk, ka-chunk. Instead, he tested me for twenty-four hours with a portable calgatator I wore on my hip. He forgot to tell me, however, that I was not supposed to mow the lawn while wearing the portable calgatator, so he was a mite concerned when he discovered that sometime the next morning, my heart rate shot up to about 344 beats per minute and stayed there for about a half an hour while I attacked what I jokingly refer to as my lawn and the neighbors call "that idiot's dandelion farm."

After I told Doc Leo that it was the lawnmower that was churning along at 344 beats per minute, he calmed down a bit and told me that some people's hearts don't always go ka-chunk. He said my bumpadas and bangadas were nothing to worry about.

I was so relieved, my heart went ka-chunk.

BURN THOSE BOOKS!

I got to thinking about public libraries the other day, about how they are filled with information that could turn our children into dangerous monsters. I think it is time we started burning books.

We need to set up a book-burning commission. Maybe even hire a book-burning consultant who will tell us which books need to be burned first, charge us a couple hundred thousand dollars, then move to Brazil.

Better still, give me a couple hundred thousand dollars, and I'll tell you right here and now which books to burn. Then I can move to Brazil and your children will be safe.

First off, we need to burn all of the sex books. There is too much sex everywhere and we need to get rid of it. If our children can't read about sex, they won't be turned into dangerous monsters.

When I was a child, my favorite sex books were my grandfather's collection of *National Geographic* magazines. They were the only books where I could find photos of bare-breasted women.

Most of those women were black, and for a while there, I thought there weren't any white women who had the guts to have their pictures taken while naked. Obviously, that was before I discovered *Playboy*. Anyway, I think we need to burn all of the old *National Geographic* magazines.

Then there are all those sex books masquerading as art books. You know the ones I mean: pornographic paintings by people like Renoir and that guy who painted all those naked Tahitians and then cut off his ear.

I'm not saying we should actually burn those perverts' paintings—just all of the "art" books in which they appear. We can keep our children from the books, and we can restrict entrance to all our art museums to adults who are over twenty-one. We can put signs on the museum doors that say: "If you were born on May 4, 1990, you can come inside and look at the pornographic paintings." Museum curators could change the date every day.

When I was a child, my favorite pornographic painting was *Persephone*, by Thomas Hart Benton. Check it out, but don't let your children see it.

We need to start burning a whole bunch of books that teach violence. All those martial arts books and the like. And I don't know about you, but I think there's an awful lot of smiting going on in the Old Testament.

I'm not saying we should burn the Old Testament. Heaven forbid. Maybe we could just clean it up a little bit and get rid of all that smiting.

I wonder if we couldn't save almost all the beautiful, proud works of humankind by cleaning them up. We might not have to burn anything. Perhaps we could paint a pink bikini on Persephone, maybe strike out every reference to smiting in the Old Testament.

We could appoint a book-*cleaning* commission, maybe even hire a book-cleaning consultant. Better yet, hire me and I'll make sure that public libraries don't turn your kids into dangerous monsters.

Instead, they'd all turn out like me.

WRITING FUNNY

I'll be the first to admit it: I am no expert on humorous writing. Most of the time I consider myself fortunate simply to put 500 words together that are coherent sentences, more or less.

My uncle Walter, on the other hand, was an expert on humorous writing. He taught for decades at the University of Chicago and wrote several books on humorous writing. But since he is quite dead, I am reasonably certain he will not quibble with what I am about to say about humorous writing.

First of all, humorous writing has to be funny. You might think that is an obvious statement, but I am here to tell you that not all humorous writing is funny.

Take one of my favorite humorous writers, Dave Barry, for example. Not all of the stuff he writes is funny.

For instance, just a couple of weeks ago, Dave Barry used the conjunction "and" in a sentence. That was not very funny, although I did chuckle simply because I am used to laughing at anything Dave Barry writes, whether or not it is funny.

Dave Barry violated the First Law of Humorous Writing. I don't think you'll find the Laws of Humorous Writing in any book, including my uncle Walter's, because I am making this stuff up as I go.

The First Law states: *If you want to write something funny, you must not offend any readers. If you offend one reader, that reader will not think you are funny.*

So Dave Barry wrote something I thought was funny, but it offended one reader. That reader thinks Dave Barry is about as funny as fleas in his underwear.

The Second Law of Humorous Writing says: *It is impossible to write anything funny without offending someone.*

Some writers who attempt humor therefore try to write stories about inanimate objects, like fire hydrants or big clumps of fungus. The problem is, for each inanimate object you write about, you will offend at least one person who takes that object very seriously. If I wrote, for example, that fire hydrants exist only to serve as mail stations for dogs, at least one fire commissioner would be offended. If I wrote that Martha Stewart was uglier than the big clump of fungus in my yard, Martha Stewart would be offended.

The Third Law of Humorous Writing is the most important of all. It says: *If it is impossible to write something without offending someone, you should offend someone who has no sense of humor.*

That is why I am always picking on planners, consultants, and emergency services coordinators. If you write something funny about people who have no sense of humor, you will have a much better chance of not offending anyone. That is because you will have offended those people long ago and they will no longer read anything you write.

In closing, I'd just like to say that if I have offended anyone other than Martha Stewart, emergency services coordinators, planners, or consultants, I am terribly sorry.

DOGGIE PLACEBO

I was afraid that Tar, the Wunderhund, had become a hypochondriac. I thought as much when I was able to heal him with a placebo.

A placebo is a pill that has absolutely no medicine in it. They cost $55 per bottle and you need a prescription.

Friends have insinuated that one of the reasons Tar feigns illness is because he subconsciously resents the fact that I always wanted a Siberian husky or a Malamute. Instead, I have a miniature poodle that I treat as if he were capable of doing all the things a husky or Malamute could do.

I don't mean I make him pull a sled or anything like that. But I do expect him to carry his own weight when we go hiking.

So I set off on a five-mile hike and Tar, who is ninety-one years old, trots along behind. When he was younger, he trotted along in front, but found so many interesting trailside scents that he could take only a few steps between stops.

Thus the hike proceeded in this fashion: take one step, step over the dog, take another step, watch the dog passing on the right, take another step, step over the dog. And so it went, for five miles.

Now, five miles is quite a distance for an animal who takes four times as many steps to cover the same territory as you do in one. I figured my dog could handle it because even if he wasn't a husky, I wanted him to be one. That is called canine denial.

As you might guess, Tar eventually hurt himself trying to meet my expectations. His back started bothering him, and he started complaining about it.

A very foolish man once tried to tell me that animals can't talk, which is pure nonsense. Anyone who has not heeded the warning growl of an angry rottweiler can refute that.

So I took Tar to the vet. The vet said Tar had a bad back and that his teeth needed cleaning, and I wrote the vet a check for $432. Then he gave Tar some pills that must be the canine equivalent of ibuprofen. One pill, and Tar became a puppy again.

The vet's nurse also told me, "The doctor has some issues with Tar's eyes." Heed my warning—when a person in the animal medical profession uses the word "issues," you had better review your portfolio, because it is going to shrink in the near future.

The vet said Tar was blind, according to the nurse. That is one reason I call him the Wunderhund, because he can catch balls and Frisbees as if he had excellent vision.

But you can't argue with medical science, so I filled the prescription for the blindness medicine, too. I wrote another check for $165.60.

Last week, Tar ran out of doggie ibuprofen. I slipped him a placebo and he turned into a puppy again—at least until the middle of the night, when he woke me up to insist I get him some real medicine.

SUMMER CAMP TIPS

I have been thinking long and hard—Hardbody says that is quite impossible, but what does she know?—about some advice for kids before they go off to their first summer camp. Kids deserve to know that boredom awaits them at Lake Slapenscratch, but I am assuming you parents have the good taste to not let them read anything I write.

Therefore, I ask you right-thinking adults to review the following. If you think it appropriate for little Missy or Junior, please share it with them. Actually, I don't mean "share." That is one of those smarmy do-gooder words that makes me puke—see, I told you to review this before "sharing" it with the kids. Anyway, here's my summer camp advice for kids. Pay attention, there's a quiz later.

First off, you've got to pick the appropriate camp. Junior: If Dad tells you the camp he's picked for you offers "three hots and a cot," tell Dad you'd rather visit your uncle Billy, even if he does that strange thing with his nose.

And Missy: When Mom suggests that Camp Camellia will be just the spot to discover the mysteries of womanhood, don't go. Fish out that case of the flu you got last March when Mom and Dad got you the date with that slimy geek who moved in next door.

I think one of the worst summer experiences (That's another one of those overused yuppie words: "Experience this. Experience that." Crap.) for teens is the National Outdoor Leadership School. I mean, you actually sweat, which causes embarrassing body odor. And as we all know, body odor is the last thing any teenager needs to get at camp. You're much better off, Missy and Junior, at one of those fuzzywarm camps where they teach you how to do your own colors.

I'd give a wide berth to any summer camp that uses words like "personal growth" or "self awareness" in its advertising. You're young, after all, and you only get to be that once every lifetime.

Instead, try to convince Mom and Dad that Camp Carefree is the place you should be this summer. Pick a camp where the lifeguards and counselors are unable to get through a sentence without using the word "like" at least eight times.

Here's the quiz. To find out if your camp is right, ask the camp boss or counselor three questions:

1. Can you have extra dessert at breakfast?

2. Does anyone play a bugle early in the morning or late at night?

3. Does each camping cabin have satellite TV or—in the case of primitive camps—cable?

If the camp boss answers "No" to the first question, "Yes" to the second, and "No" to the third, you have only one choice. When it comes time to go to camp, call in sick.

Heck, if your Mom and Dad can do it, why shouldn't you?

DO AS LITTLE AS POSSIBLE

Despite the fact that many of you will not read this, and, I'm afraid, not a few of you will be incapable of reading, I have decided to give you graduates some advice you will get here and nowhere else. If you are not a graduate or have never been one, you may disregard the rest of this and move on to more meaningful reading material.

Many of you graduates will be wondering: What do I do now? This is a perfectly logical question, and you will be given many perfectly logical answers to that question in the coming weeks; answers given by politicians and government officials invited to speak at your graduation ceremonies. I say you've already spent too much time on logic and now you should consider something that is completely illogical for the rest of your life:

Do as little as possible.

This advice has served me well most of my six decades on earth.

I must caution you, however, that doing as little as possible is not likely to make you healthy, wealthy, and wise. Especially wealthy. If you want to be wealthy while still doing as little as possible, you should become a planner, a consultant, or an emergency services coordinator. You could shadow a planner, a consultant, or an emergency services coordinator for three or four months and still not figure out exactly what they do—unless there's a natural disaster.

In that case, if you are a planner or a consultant, you will deny you had any hand in the plan or consultation about the building, shopping center, or city that has just collapsed. If you choose to become an emergency services coordinator, you can still do as little as possible if you have many hard-working assistants who heeded all that other graduation advice.

That brings me to the next piece of graduation advice nobody else will give you: If you want to do as little as possible and still be wealthy, you must surround yourself with hard-working assistants. Learn to spot the graduates who pay attention to the advice they are given, and you will find yourself a hard-working assistant.

Another thing: You must at all costs avoid becoming a hard-working assistant. You can do this by refusing to accept any responsibility for anything that is wrong and taking the credit for everything that is right. You will discover that the wealthiest people who do as little as possible will tell you they have never done anything that is wrong. On the other hand, hard-working assistants frequently accept responsibility for doing something wrong. Sometimes they are so hard-working they accept responsibility for something somebody who does absolutely nothing has done wrong. I hope that last sentence makes sense to you, because for the life of me, I can't figure out what I just wrote.

Finally—and this is by far the most important piece of advice you'll get from me—you must learn how to laugh. Contrary to what others may tell you, learning to laugh is very hard work. It takes years of dedicated study.

The most peculiar thing about learning to laugh—even though it is very hard work—is that you can do it and still do absolutely nothing.

DR. RUTH, MY TEACHER

Years ago, I learned most of everything I needed to know by watching that old TV personality, Dr. Ruth. I never admitted to watching her, and told B.B. Hardbody I had turned it on by mistake.

Anyway, Dr. Ruth was giving advice on this TV talk show to parents whose children are entering college. It could be traumatic for them as well as for you, Mom and Dad.

Dr. Ruth said that Mom and Dad should take extra care to talk to little Junior and Missy, and to make certain the kids understood they might feel lonely during the first weeks of college. The TV talk show hostess told Dr. Ruth that when she was in college, her roommate got so homesick she cried incessantly. Dr. Ruth said it was good the TV hostess was a cold and calculating bitch so she didn't blubber like a baby, too.

Dr. Ruth said parents need to assure their children that besides feeling lonely, they might experience a loss of identity. She explained that most children at home get some form of attention—even if it is only Dad or Mom bugging on them to haul out the garbage or clean their rooms. At college, nobody is going to give you that sort of attention.

So Junior and Missy begin to feel just like numbers. They are simply digits in a CD, pixels in a photo. It is much the same as the rest of us feel most of the time.

I thought all of the advice Dr. Ruth gave was excellent. She is a Dr., after all.

But I was disappointed that Dr. Ruth didn't say squat to you new college students. It was like, "Even though you're on your own now, I'm going to talk to your parents."

But don't worry. I've jotted down a few thoughts for those of you who are entering college. They are based on my long and illustrious career as a college student, which I should point out was cut short when Mom and Dad destroyed my credit cards.

They thought thirty-five was a little too old to be switching majors. They figured a guy who entered college at seventeen should have gotten it together in eighteen years. Anyway, you can see that I know something about being a college student. So let me offer the following advice to you first-year college students:

I'll bet you are having a great time. If not, have a great time.

There are still some fools out there who insist that you have to go to class to learn something at college. That is patently ridiculous.

Look at me. I went to college for eighteen years, but attended classes for only three. And I learned plenty.

I learned how to drive a go-kart, how to jump on a trampoline, how to drink copious amounts of beer without having to pee. I learned a bunch of other stuff, too, but it would probably just bore you.

Besides, if I told you, you wouldn't have any fun learning it for yourself. And if you don't have fun learning, there's little point in it.

THE "R" WORD

Recession. There, I said it.

Recession, recession, recession! I am not worried in the slightest, I told B.B. Hardbody.

She wondered why, then, I was thinking about adding twenty stories to our house. The simplest answer to that is I may not die if I jump out of a second-story window.

A whole bunch of people are using the "R" word these days—and I do not mean "Reality." If my mother were alive today, she would use the "D" word. "D" is for "Depression."

People were jumping out of twenty-story windows back then. My mother would be yodeling with glee if she were alive today, because she just knew that sooner or later, we would suffer another recession, or maybe even another Great Depression. My parents were so depressed by the Great Depression that they did not take their savings out of the mattress until 1965. Dad then invested the entire $27.50 in Certificates of Deposit, which at the time were earning a whopping 2 percent interest, compounded every decade.

"You'll see," they told me. "You just can't trust the stock market. You'll lose everything."

I tried to explain to them that the stock market had changed since the 1920s, and that it would be impossible to lose money today. "Why, all you have to do today is buy low and sell high. Everybody's doing it," I said.

My mother's answer to that was, "If everybody cut off their big toe, would you?"

"I am not worried," I repeated to B.B. Hardbody. "My Nest Egg has already been fried and scrambled." I called Vinnie, my financial advisor at the National Bank of Usury, to ask what I should do to save my Nest Egg. He liked the twenty-story idea.

"Normally," Vinnie said, "I would advise you to buy low and sell high. But as you have no money with which to buy low, I'm not at all confident you would be able to sell high."

I don't blame Vinnie for frying and scrambling my Nest Egg. There was this mutual fund, "All or Nothin' " that the Bank of Usury was offering. It looked good to me, 83 percent return each of the last five years, and I wanted in.

"Normally," Vinnie said, "I would say that the All or Nothin' Fund has tremendous growth potential. But you must remember that if we experience the 'R' word, you will go down the tube faster than a bottle of Fleet soda."

But I would have none of it. I jumped into the All or Nothin' Fund like it was a big bowl of chocolate–peanut butter cups. Things went swell for a couple of months. I began to feel guilty about making money without working for it.

That is a silly Puritan concept, I know. There are hundreds of thousands of people out there making money who don't work for it. I'll bet you can name a few where you toil.

I'm not worried now. I've discovered I can lose money without actually working, too.

II. B.B. HARDBODY AND ME

HALF A BRAIN

"There is a logical reason why men listen with only half their brains," I told B.B. Hardbody. My wife was showing me the study that said unlike men, women listen with both sides of their brains.

"What's that?" she asked.

"Men only need half a brain to figure out the simplistic stuff women are always talking about."

Hardbody suggested I might be more comfortable sleeping in the tool shed for the rest of my life. ("There's no room," I argued. "Sleep on the table saw," she said.)

I didn't think she was giving me the whole story about how men and women listen, so I read the story myself. Sure enough, it turns out the whole study was biased. For example, the ten male and ten female subjects listened to a John Grisham novel. No wonder men listened with only half their brains—John Grisham writes all that sensitive renaissance crap that only appeals to women.

"How would you know what John Grisham writes?" Hardbody said. "You've never read anything by him. I'll bet the last book you read was *Dick and Jane Meet Spot* in second grade."

My retort was too clever and subtle for her: "Hah! I've read plenty of books."

Now, if they'd just listened to something written by Zane Gray, or maybe the woman who does the weather report on the NFL FOX pre-game show, it would be a different story. You can bet every man in the universe would be listening with a whole lot more than both sides of his brain.

The study showed women listened with the left and right sides of their brains, while men listened with only with the left. "That shows that with women, it goes in one ear and out the other," I said.

"I'm relatively certain you don't have the slightest idea of what you are talking about," Hardbody said. (Actually, she said nothing of the sort—but if I wrote what she really said here, you'd just roll your eyes and say something about vulgarity in print.)

I told Hardbody about the conversation between two women sitting behind me on the ferry the other day. "It was so banal I didn't have to use either side of my brain to listen," I said.

"I'm worried about Dawn and Brian," one woman had said.

"Me, too," said the other. "Do you think Gloria or George knows about them?"

"I don't know. But I know that Mary and Mike know."

"I didn't know Mary and Mike knew. But I knew Bobbie and Bill did."

"I didn't know that."

See, that's the kind of pap women listen to with both sides of their brain. No wonder men don't hear half the stuff women say—it's not worth listening to. My theory, I told Hardbody, is that men use one side of their brain to store vital information, like how to change a flat tire. Women discard all that information because they know men will always be there when they get a flat tire.

Then I noticed Hardbody had left the room. She didn't even do me the courtesy of listening with half her brain.

MIGRATING OBJECTS

The Theory of Migrating Objects came to me in a flash of gestalten insight you might call genius. I was loading for a four-day backpack when it hit me: Things never stay where you put them. They migrate.

"Have you seen my water bottle?" I asked B.B. Hardbody.

"Yeah—but I can't remember where," she lied.

Women always know where things migrate. That is a key postulate to the Theory of Migrating Objects.

Women don't tell you because they want to see you scrabbling around the house, emptying drawers you haven't opened in twelve years, searching for your water bottle. Then, after you have given up and are lying glazen-eyed on the floor, panting and wheezing, they go to the shelf where you keep your bicycle gear and pull out your water bottle.

"Here it is," says B.B. Though she tries to hide it, I can tell that she is smirking.

"You're smirking," I say.

"No, I've got hay fever," she lies. The only time she gets hay fever is when one of my objects migrates and she finds it. That is an axiom to the Theory.

Now, I am certain I know where I put the water bottle the last time I used it. I put it into my day-pack, which is at least three Gorilla rack shelves below my bike gear. Sometime between then and now—I suspect it is the middle of the night because I hear things moving around—the water bottle has migrated up three shelves.

The Theory of Migrating Objects states that you will find the object in precisely the spot you are positive it is not. My water bottle could not possibly be on the bike gear shelf, because I have a bike water bottle and there is little point in putting my hiking water bottle there.

Thus the only plausible explanation is that the bottle migrated by itself. The Theory solves a host of mysteries, as you can see.

You've probably misplaced your car keys, for example. You search everywhere but the place they couldn't possibly be and finally ask the woman in your life if she's seen your keys.

She says she has seen them, but can't remember where. Then she goes and finds them. Women intuitively know that objects migrate to the spot they couldn't possibly be, and women know exactly where that spot is.

I tried to explain the Theory of Migrating Objects to B. B. Hardbody, but I'm pretty certain it was too complicated for her simple mind. "Are you telling me," she asks, "that you think inanimate objects move in the middle of the night?"

"That's the only possible way my hiking water bottle could get on the bike shelf."

"Perhaps," she says, with that hay-fever look, "or maybe the guy who wanted an extra water bottle for the long bike ride last week left it with the bike gear."

Big deal. That still doesn't explain why women are always finding your car keys.

CALL ME JACK

I am not one to brag upon my culinary skills in the kitchen or, for that matter, any other room of the house. This is due in part to my dislike of braggarts; possibly more because those who have culinary skills will instantly discern from the following that I have none.

You may remember that my constant companion, Stummick, has been growling about my trying the Atkins Diet, so I have become a "Jack" Atkins dieter. That is to say, I eat all the stuff Dr. Atkins allows, plus all the stuff he doesn't.

Stuff like pasta. Bread. Potatoes. Sixty-three pounds of Reese's I made certain were left over from Halloween.

B.B. Hardbody, on the other hand, follows the Atkins regime so strictly that if you wave a piece of rigatoni in her direction, she runs screaming from the room. The very word "carbohydrate" sends her reeling.

As you might guess, our differing interpretations of the Atkins rules have stressed our domestic tranquility.

I prepared one of Hardbody's favorite desserts—cheesecake—as a peace offering. When made without the graham cracker crust, using phony sugar, a cheesecake has practically no carbohydrates.

The recipe follows:

1 envelope unflavored gelatine
1/2 cup phony sugar
2 (8-ounce) packages of cream cheese, softened
1 cup boiling water
1 teaspoon vanilla extract

1. Mix gelatine and phony sugar in a small bowl. Make certain the gelatine envelope paper is not inadvertently dropped into the bowl. Believe me, once you dump the boiling water in there, the paper is extremely difficult and painful to remove.

2. Beat cream cheese and vanilla in a large bowl with a mixer until smooth. Do not attempt to soften the cream cheese in your microwave, especially if you forgot to remove the aluminum foil wrapping. This can cause a serious mess that can take at least forty-five minutes to clean up and possibly damage your microwave.

Another thing—never lift a mixer operating at high speed from the large bowl when the beaters are clogged with half-softened cream cheese. The whirling beaters have an annoying habit of distributing cream cheese throughout various parts of your kitchen, perhaps on your household pet, and beyond.

3. Slowly beat in the gelatine mixture. You now have twenty seconds until the whole mess turns to concrete in the bowl.

4. Pour the mixture into a nine-inch pie pan lined with stretch wrap. If, like me, you are a Jack Atkins dieter, dump the stuff into a prepared graham cracker crust or—better still—dump the stuff in the garbage and run to the store for one of Sara Lee's really nummy cheesecakes.

5. Refrigerate until firm, about three hours. Garnish as desired. A good Atkins-friendly garnish would be cherry-flavored whipped cream, sweetened with phony sugar.

6. Wait until B.B. Hardbody arrives home to discover that a rather large splot of partially softened, microwaved cream cheese has somehow migrated from the kitchen to lodge itself smack in the middle of the TV screen in the living room.

FLU SUCKS

B.B. Hardbody has the flu. She is a pathetic sight: awash in a mound of tissue paper, pale as a snowdrift, coughing like an outboard motor that hasn't been started since last fall.

I try to cheer her up. "Good morning, Starshine," I say.

She moans and throws an empty box of tissue at me. It is an excellent measure of how really sick she is that the box bounces off the wall rather than putting a hole in the plasterboard.

I've been incredibly lucky. Please find some wood and knock on it for me. I haven't got the flu yet.

In fact, I haven't had a case of the flu since 1978, which, curiously enough, is the last year I had a flu shot. Those of you who assume that I am a very healthy dude should know that my blood pressure is around 600 over 220 and that it is impossible to check my cholesterol because bacon fat runs in my veins.

My guess is that any flu bug that gets near me takes one look and decides it would be a good deal healthier for it to go infect somebody else. Any flu bug in my body could die before it killed me.

The last time I had the flu, I decided to call the doctor. That was back in the days before cordless phones, so I had to crawl out of the bedroom and down the stairs to the telephone.

This took me exactly five days and by the time I got to the bottom of the stairs, the sickness had run its course and I was feeling well enough to stop at the refrigerator and get a snack. It was the first solid food I had eaten since I crawled up the stairs to bed, ten days earlier.

I suggested to B.B. Hardbody that she visit her doctor. She was fresh out of tissue boxes to throw, so she agreed. The receptionist at her doctor's office told Hardbody on the phone that she could see the doctor in five days, which would be OK if she were going to crawl, but I said I'd drive her.

"That would be very nice, I'm sure," said B.B., "but I'm not entirely certain I'll be alive five days from now." (Actually, Hardbody said nothing of the sort, but I wouldn't dare repeat what she really said.)

I am saddened by the fact that so many people suffer from the flu that doctors have a five-day waiting list. It is bad enough to feel like you have just been run down by a semi truck and trailer and that it is now speeding down your throat to your lungs, but waiting five days to see someone who might make you feel better really sucks.

The five-day wait does little to cheer B.B., as you might guess. She crawls off to bed, burrowing deeper under her mound of tissue paper.

I wonder if doctors ever get the flu. I wonder if they wait five days before they can see someone who might make them feel better.

BIKE REPAIR 101

B.B. Hardbody is becoming intolerable. We attended a basic bicycle repair class and the instructor showed us how to clean a chain and lubricate a fabiter.

The instructor asked, "Now, has everybody got that?"

B.B. Hardbody said, "You'd better explain that again to Mr. Outdoors. His eyes are glazed."

I attempted to explain that my eyes most certainly were not glazed. My contact lenses tend to fog when I am trying to think too hard.

As I said, Hardbody is becoming intolerable. I decided to get even by taking her on a mountain bike ride. B.B. wanted me to lubricate our fabiters, but I would have none of her excuses. We took off up the trail, about ten miles of single-track torture. In the first place, you've got to dodge trees. They sprout from seedlings to massive Douglas fir in a matter of seconds.

Trees are the least of your worries. There are rocks—nay, boulders the size of Volkswagens—which appear on the trail in front of you as if Scotty, on the *Enterprise*, had just pushed the Energize button.

"Gosh," B.B. said as she gathered various parts of my body from a boulder, "I thought you saw that. Are you sure your contacts aren't fogged again?"

I was careful on the trail to yield to hikers. This is part of the mountain bikers' Code of Ethics. At one point, I pulled over onto some weeds off the trail to let a couple of hikers walk by. Hardbody rode past me and around the hikers, leaving them plenty of room. One of the hikers giggled as she walked by me.

"Don't you know that poison oak grows along this trail?" she asked. But she did not wait for my reply. If she had, she would have heard me say that of course I know that poison oak grows along this trail. After all, she was talking to Mr. Outdoors.

So I'm sitting there, or at least I think I'm sitting there (you can never be certain after you've been on a mountain bike for more than five minutes) and B.B. Hardbody rides back to me. She looks at me sitting there, or thinking I'm sitting there.

"Do you know you're in a bunch of poison oak?"

She chortles and snorks like a blender full of English walnuts. I am beginning to itch worse than a barber's used apron.

The end of the trail is within reach. I believe I have not harmed my reproductive system by sitting on a mountain bike for almost two hours. Two feet from the end of the trail, my bicycle—the Great Emasculator—gets tired of letting me ride it and decides to ride me. It flips me over on my back like a drunken turtle and slams down upon me.

"Gawd," says B.B. "I look away for one second, and you fall over."

I try to insist that this would not have happened if only she had let me lubricate our fabiters, but she just chortles and snorks again.

MOUNTAIN BIKING: GETTING EVEN

B.B. Hardbody is riding her Raleigh gingerly these days, the result of a winter of neglect. If you stay off of a mountain bike saddle for three months, you can actually begin to feel pain below your waist once again.

That Hardbody is experiencing pain is a source of joy to me. It is in some small way retribution for all of the abuse I have taken at her hands recently. For example:

I am building two sawhorses to hold up the Bigfoot truck camper when it is off the truck. She sticks her head out the door and asks: "Shall I warn the neighbors you're using power tools again?"

My sawhorses are excellent examples of my awesome handyman's talent. I had some difficulty figuring out how to build them, however, so I visited the friendly folks at my favorite do-it-yourself store, Glue This! They tried unsuccessfully to explain the concept to me for about ninety minutes, and finally one of them handed me a box.

"Here, try these. They're metal."

"How will I nail them together?" I asked.

Then I visited the friendly folks at the RV store, and they sold me a set of camper tie-downs. Unless you want your truck camper to travel south when the rest of your party is traveling north, camper tie-downs are a good idea. The folks at the RV store are well aware of my mechanical genius, because I have bought many doodads and framises there before.

"Are you sure you can recognize a wrench?" they asked.

I took my new tie-downs home and the first thing Hardbody said was, "This thing's bolted on. Hold the wrench by this end and twist it." She snorted like a horse in a field of alfalfa. It made me sick.

The best thing to do in situations like these is to get your detractor into a position where you can embarrass them horribly in public. So I suggested we blow the dust off the mountain bikes and ride some really easy stuff. Then I found the steepest gravel road I could and we rode up it. But B.B.'s groans after the ride weren't anywhere near loud enough. If I was going to enjoy the weekend, I had to figure out something else just short of getting her to fall off the bike and break something.

So I took her on a thirty-mile ride into a canyon. I didn't tell her about the hills. I didn't tell her about the 100-degree heat. I didn't tell her about the sandpaper I wanted to hide in her bike shorts.

As it happened, I didn't need the sandpaper. The hills and the heat were enough to cause her considerable discomfort. Even pain. It was a perfect weekend.

The new camper tie-downs work perfectly. They keep the Bigfoot from going south while we travel north. I had a few minor mechanical details to work out, like why my wrench won't work on a Phillips nut.

Hardbody says I am a Phillips nut. But she still can't sit down without flinching.

III.   HOME AND GARDEN

THE GARAGE SALE

It has only recently come to my attention that I have led a sheltered life. It is a life so sheltered that I held my very first garage sale only one week ago.

I once helped out on someone else's garage sale. But I gave away pieces of junk I could not believe anyone would pay for, so was invited to stop helping. B.B. Hardbody helped with my garage sale, which was a good thing. She is a garage sale veteran and knows all of the tricks for holding a good sale, like making really good garage sale signs and posting them all over the universe.

Unlike many who hold garage sales, we were careful to take down most of our signs after the sale. Some helpful folks—perhaps it was the fellow who missed my bargain price on a marine battery by only seconds— even took down some of Hardbody's signs for us. There are those two signs we posted off I-90, just west of De Borgia, Montana—but we'll pick them up soon. I also plan to hire mercenaries to remove the signs I put up along the Alaska Highway. These surpass the distance-from-event record set by Wall Drug, Butchart Gardens, and Harrah's signs of the past several decades.

As a newcomer, I was fascinated by the items that sold first. I figured the good stuff—the antiques and old furniture at rock-bottom prices—would sell first. But some of that never found a home and continues to cultivate mold and moss for my weed garden. No, the first thing to sell was an old wooden barrel. Minutes later, a white-haired matron paid big bucks for my rubber mold of dog poop that has never really fooled anyone.

Another thing I found most interesting were the people who showed up at my sale. Among the first was a leather-clad professional garage saler who carried a wad of money in one hand and a black bullwhip in the other to fend off the competition.

She cruised the aisles at about thirty-five miles per hour, mowing anyone down who crossed her path. "Hey, Little Bit," she addressed me, "got the table with this set of antique chairs?"

"Sorry," I said, "it's not for sale."

"That's not the right answer, Bozo," she said. I believe she intended to pull out my fingernails, one by one, until I agreed to sell the table—but a kindly old gentleman with one tooth interrupted to ask how much I wanted for the rubber cement ball I painstakingly constructed during the thirty years I was supposed to be working at the office.

Another early bird dropped by to say how disappointed he was in the quality of merchandise I was offering. "If I were looking for crap like this," he said, "I'd have gone to Restoration Hardware."

That was particularly amusing to me, because I bought a lot of the crap I was selling from Restoration Hardware.

WANTED: ONE DO-IT-YOURSELFER

I've said it before and I'll say it again: I am not a Do-It-Yourselfer. I am a Find-Somebody-Who-Knows-What-They're-Doinger.

There is a saying: "If it isn't broken, don't fix it." You may think it good advice and you may be right. But consider this: If it's broken, wait a while and a Do-It-Yourselfer will come along and fix it for you. For example, a Do-It-Yourselfer helped me build a new deck because another acquaintance fell through the old deck at my house at Lake Slimeington. He was the second person to fall through the old deck and the Do-It-Yourselfer figured it was only a matter of time before he fell through.

While I am not a Do-It-Yourselfer, I am probably a world-class Break-It-Yourselfer. I can pretty much break anything I want, often without the help of special tools. Sometimes you have to use special tools. There was that time, not so very long ago, that I had to use my Bigfoot camper to break the lid of my septic tank.

My friend Skip the Scott (husband to Sharon the Strong) is a great DIYer. He builds beautiful hardwood furniture, and if I allowed it, he would take my list of 6,134 DIY projects and do them himself.

That is probably the best thing about Do-It-Yourselfers. They've done everything around their house, so they look for Find-Somebody-Who-Knows-What-They're-Doingers. The household with DIYer friends is blessed, indeed.

B.B. Hardbody, who some noseysmarts say is "my better half," is a DIYer. She does stuff I mainly don't understand, like hooking rugs. She understands the intricacies of using contact paper to line drawers. She would watch Martha Stewart if—as she often says—Martha Stewart didn't make her puke.

The other day, I did an incredible thing for an FSWKWTDer. I painted the kitchen without help, even from Hardbody or Skip the Scott. I went to my favorite DIY store, Glue This! It is an amazing store, with more than 850,000 square feet of DIY stuff. It is open twenty-four hours a day, and at any given time, you will find at least 350 people wandering vacant-eyed and drooling down the aisles. You can practically see the little balloon dreams above their head:

"*. . . a new hot tub where that scummy shower is . . .*"

"*. . . Mediterranean tile in the laundry room . . .*"

"*. . . Somebody else to paint the kitchen . . .*" Ooops, sorry. That was my dream balloon.

Vinnie, the paint salesperson, said that if I was going to paint the kitchen, I would need a couple of gallons of semi-gloss enamel. I told him my better half didn't like semi-gloss enamel.

"I suppose she doesn't like Martha Stewart, either," said Vinnie. "If you are anti-semi-gloss, Martha Stewart makes you puke."

Vinnie said that if I matched the color perfectly to the walls in the hallway, Hardbody would never know the new paint was semi-gloss. I took his word for it: If you can't trust a Glue This! salesperson, who can you trust? The paint came to $32.50. I paid an extra $50 for a roll of masking plastic with its own sticky stuff. A word to DIYers: Do not attempt to put the masking plastic on inside-out.

The first thing Hardbody said when she saw my handiwork was, "That looks like semi-gloss enamel to me."

I've said it before and I'll say it again: I am not a Do-It-Yourselfer.

ADVICE FROM RICKY

After nearly six decades of intensive and sometimes painful study, I have concluded it is impossible to please a woman. Counselors told me that during one of those painful times, but counselors will say anything to make a buck.

Those of you to take umbrage, or perhaps offense, at the preceding slam should ask yourself: "What am I paying counselors for?" The answer is, to tell you what is wrong with you.

Anyway, they are correct about pleasing other people. You can only please yourself. But it has taken me nearly six decades to figure it out, even after Ricky Nelson told me in "Garden Party" 5,000 years ago. Don't try to please others unless it pleases you.

A recent case in point is the gutters on my house at Lake Slimeington, Rising Waters. B.B. Hardbody has been "suggesting" for at least nine years that I clean the gutters. Now, I have seen no reason to clean the gutters. They have sprouted a healthy crop of fireweed that grows faster and healthier than the stuff sprouting around the big stump in my moss garden out front.

A small fir tree took root in the south gutter, next to

an alder and two fine Scotch Broom plants my neighbor imported from far away on his bulldozer track. Grass goes to seed in the north gutter and, as many of you know, I consider grass the ultimate weed.

You've got to mow it, for God's sake, and feed it, and protect it from other plants that grow without requiring attention. Like women, you can't please turf.

But I still had not learned, so I decided to please B.B. Hardbody and clean the gutters. On the rainiest day of the century, I went outside to clean the gutters. Ducks were drowning on the front moss garden, and I was slogging around with a ladder and a garden trowel. The gutters had gathered more good organic topsoil in nine years than you could find at a Home Depot nursery. A small Kubota garden tractor would have made quicker work out of the task. But all I had was the garden trowel.

I dug up the fir, alder, and Scotch Broom on the south side and the grass in the north gutter. I found a flourishing cranberry bog in the northwest corner, which the builder of my house, Rising Waters, had cleverly installed below the level of the drain at the northeast corner.

The builder of Rising Waters also somehow knew the width of my hand. He overlapped the gutter with abrasive roofing exactly one-quarter inch narrower than the width of my hand.

Both the gutter-cleaning and the rain lasted all day. By evening, I was as water-wrinkled as an albino prune, my hands bloody stumps.

I dribbled my way inside, where B.B. Hardbody was warm and dry. "I cleaned the gutters for you," I said.

"Does that make you happy?"

"You dewhead," she said. "You just ruined the best garden you ever had."

See what I mean? You can't please a woman.

GROOVING ON LUMBER

I have long considered tongue and groove lumber to be an invention equal to the computer to the survival of our galaxy. But now I wonder.

Tongue and groove lumber is the yin and the yang of woodworking. Take two pieces of wood and glue them together. The joint stands out like a ferry boat in the Mojave, heh?

Now take a piece of wood with a nubbin of a bump along one side and another piece of wood with a groove along one side. Gluing them together is as easy as slipping on a banana peel. That's the advantage of tongue and groove lumber. It sticks together to form a joint that is virtually invisible.

Many of my best do-it-yourself projects were a success simply because I used tongue and groove lumber. If you've got a project that you'd like to try this summer—a deck or a potting shed or maybe a kennel for your spouse—you should try building it with tongue and groove lumber.

There is only one piece of wood that is superior to tongue and groove, and that is what the experts call "end-matched." End-matched lumber has a tongue on two adjoining sides and a groove on the other two sides.

This means that a woodworker can join three or more pieces of wood together and you will not be able to see the joint. At least, that is the way it works with experts.

Recently, I got myself about $1,200 worth of end-matched lumber—hardwood maple flooring—and discovered that even end-matched tongue and groove lumber in the hands of a complete idiot is worth little more than a toothpick. In fact, if you know anyone who would like some quality maple toothpicks, please let me know.

I went down to see Vinnie, my favorite salesperson at Glue This!, the discount do-it-yourself store. He showed me a product called "laminate flooring," and said that just about anybody could put it down for a delightful hardwood-floor look. It was easy, he said, because all of the pieces were tongue and groove and end-matched. "You can get a whole new floor in just one weekend," Vinnie said.

Gophers and moles are beginning to invade my carpet, so I decided to install a new hardwood floor. I bought the stuff from Vinnie and carted it home, where B.B. Hardbody informed me that within a couple of days, she was certain we would have next winter's firewood. Big deal. I had Skip the Scott, a friend and expert woodworker, to help if I needed. And tongue and groove had never failed me before.

So I set to, laying down plank like John Henry building a railroad. When I finished, there was a whole lot of groove showing and precious little tongue.

I'm now thankful that I have discovered a new product, which I am certain is at least as great as the computer when it comes to significance to humanity. It is called "wood filler."

CAN YOU HEAR ME NOW?

It is beginning to feel like I am the only person in the universe without a cell phone. B. B. Hardbody has a cell phone. So does my friend, The Gnarly Dude.

Hardbody hardly ever uses her cell phone. But that does not stop her from charging it, then letting the battery run down until it beeps plaintively from underneath a pile of books and papers on her desk. The Dude uses his cell phone constantly. We recently returned from a road trip to Fernie and Kimberley, B.C., where he used—or tried to use—his cell phone as often as you click your mouse when shopping online.

Kimberley and Fernie, B.C., by the way, are two of the best spots in the known universe to ski or ride a snowboard. That is why we visited there. From what I hear, the golfing at Kimberley and the fly fishing at Fernie are world-class, too. But as the only thing I catch with a fly is my ear, and golfing to me is about as exciting as watching an ice cube melt, I wouldn't know.

Kimberley and Fernie didn't have a whole lot of snow when we visited. That changed later, but what little snow they did have put massive smiles on our faces. When The Dude was not skiing, he was talking on his cell phone. Sometimes he talked and skied at the same time. He talked to three separate people in one single ride up the chair lift at Kimberley.

He spent most of the time in Fernie talking to the friendly folks at the phone company via landline about why he could not talk on his cell phone. It seems his cell phone thought it was in Kalispell, Montana, when it was actually in Fernie, and no amount of electronic prodding could convince it otherwise.

One night, The Dude talked to the friendly folks at the phone company for two hours and thirty minutes, trying to convince them to convince his cell phone that it was not in Kalispell. The friendly folks at the phone company told him to try various things, such as standing on his head in the hot tub, but nothing would convince his cell phone that it was not in Kalispell.

Once we arrived in Kimberley, however, the phone figured out where it was and The Dude made up for all that lost telephone time by calling as many people as he could. That phone message on your answering machine—the one that was silent—was probably The Dude. I suggested that perhaps The Dude was making all those phone calls simply to justify the cost of his cell phone. But The Dude said it was important to check skiing conditions at thirty-five other wintersports areas, even though we were skiing in Kimberley.

The Dude was even kind enough to let me use his cell phone a couple of times. I tried to call B.B. Hardbody, but of course, her batteries were dead.

NOXIOUS WEEDS

Last week, I launched my seasonal attack on what little healthy turf remains on my beautiful moss lawn. I mulched dandelions, brambles, and—ATTENTION! NOXIOUS WEED BOARD—what I am fairly certain is ragweed over my turf, hoping to kill it before winter.

Perhaps you remember I have carefully cultivated my moss lawn for almost a year now, and I am happy to report almost all of the turf has yielded to some truly remarkable moss. There was that large patch of healthy turf growing in my house gutter, but I ripped it out last summer. The best way to get rid of those lingering blades of grass, I have discovered, is to mow them down. I haul out Grass Gobbler, my 3.5-horsepower mower, and attack.

Grass Gobbler was B.B. Hardbody's favorite mower before I got ahold of it. I was mowing the community park and ran into a boulder, which so bent the blade that it jammed on the shaft, making it impossible to remove or even sharpen. At least, that is the story I insist is true. Hardbody gave up on Grass Gobbler shortly thereafter and the mower's blade is now so dull that it no longer cuts, but merely beats the weeds until they break.

Like, Grass Gobbler ran into a big banana slug the other day and *Ariolimax columbianus* emerged with only bruises and contusions. I find that slugs thrive on healthy turf and flower gardens, so I try to keep as many of the mollusks around as I can without risking frivolous lawsuits from visitors who might slip on one on my front steps.

Slugs are really quite interesting creatures. Did

you know that some species of mushroom spores must pass through the digestive system of a slug before the mushrooms can regenerate? Think about that the next time you sauté those chanterelles. I didn't know slugs ate mushroom spores until I read the first edition of Ann Saling's *Great Northwest Nature Factbook*. I was particularly interested in the slug's sex life, which is much too disgusting to relate here. Suffice it to say that slugs are hermaphroditic, which as near as I can figure means they are both male and female, so it must be terribly confusing.

But as I was saying, I attacked what remains of my turf with Grass Gobbler. I adjust the beating bar at the lowest possible setting, which gouges most of the lingering grass out by the roots and spreads my glorious moss across the bald spot that remains. This method of mowing also has an added benefit. It levels off most of the mounds in my yard, left by fertilizer hillocks where such ugly plants as roses, rhododendrons, and azaleas once grew.

Don't get the mistaken notion that I hate flowers. I have a fine fireweed garden, which reminds Hardbody of her beloved Alaska. And there is nothing more beautiful than a dandelion patch going to seed.

But I don't think my neighbors appreciate my green thumb.

LOVE AT SECOND SIGHT

I have fallen in love, once again. In times past, when I fell in love, it often was with people who did not fall in love with me. Many of them, in fact, were complete strangers.

That is not a problem this time. This time I have fallen in love with an inanimate object. Before you go snidely snickering to yourself, I should assure you that the object I have fallen in love with is not inflatable. Far from it; I have fallen in love with ProBond Wood Filler. Unlike many of my previous loves, ProBond Wood Filler won't crack or shrink, has a fast drying time, and is stainable and sandable. Further, it is put together with Professional Elmer's Strength and can now be purchased in a new easy-spread formula.

You could read that all on the label. What you will not read on the label—what is most important in this love story—is how I came to fall in love with ProBond Wood Filler.

It all began when the woman I love, who is not a complete stranger, came home the other day from work and asked, "Don't you think it's a little late to be sleeping in?" I explained to B.B. Hardbody that I was working. Sometimes the best way to get an idea for something to write about is to go to sleep. Your subconscious mind will give you ideas, I told B.B.

"My subconscious mind is giving me ideas," she said. "You don't want to know what they are."

She wanted me to help her move this spiffy new Amish bedroom set she bought. It is splendid woodwork, handcrafted by people who don't drive automobiles.

The big problem with the new furniture is that I had to build a television stand to match it. That meant using power tools, which I am forbidden to handle without chain metal gloves and adult supervision.

So I got out my new table saw and some extra maple plank hardwood flooring I found from the last woodworking job I never finished, and got to work. I sawed this way and that, and finally got a piece that was reasonably square—that is to say, it was more square than round—and made a TV stand out of it. It needed edges, so I visited Vinnie, the salesperson at Glue This!, my favorite discount hardware store. He sold me some hardwood edging that cost more than our TV.

"Here, you should take some of this," he said, tossing a can of ProBond Wood Filler into my basket. "You can never tell when you might need it."

Indeed. I went home and sawed this way and that for a while, finally getting some edging that was more or less the correct size. That is when I fell in love.

Because today I have a ten-piece TV stand that is one part hardwood maple and nine parts ProBond Wood Filler.

MOSS MANIA

Martha Stewart probably already knows this, but here's an important piece of information for those of you who—like me—view horticulture as second only to embalming as a hobby. Moss never grows where you want it to grow.

For several years now, I've been trying to get moss to replace what is left of the grass on my lawn. Moss is so much more maintenance-free than grass; it never needs mowing and is a healthy green all year long, even if you don't water it. In fact, if all of the lawns in the country were replaced by moss, we could save enough water to light both Las Vegas and Los Angeles for the rest of the decade. Keeping electricity flowing to Las Vegas and Los Angeles seems to be a priority; I don't know why.

Anyway, I've tried some great moss recipes: buttermilk and blendered moss seems to work the best for transplanting most types of the green stuff. Trouble is, the dandelions and other noxious weeds I've been cultivating appear to dominate the moss. I have seen dandelions standing over the moss in their skin-tight leather suits, whips at the ready. You may feel free to disbelieve me if you choose.

Regardless, the moss I am trying to cultivate doesn't seem to like my noxious weeds. Instead, it has migrated to my concrete driveway and my roof, of all places. On the roof—and I'm guessing Martha Stewart would have an accurate answer about this—the moss appears to have no natural enemy. In fact, it appears to thrive on asphalt shingles, and no matter how much I coax and beg, my moss will not come down off the roof and mix it up with the weeds and what remains of my lawn.

You might understand why moss grows on roofs, especially if you watch Martha Stewart, but I'm not certain anyone can explain why it grows on my concrete driveway. It gets crushed at least twice daily by my truck, the Belching Beast (a name I have borrowed

from one of B.B. Hardbody's endearments for me)—
and Hardbody routinely lays rubber on the stuff when
she heads to work.

Still it thrives. It creeps along the cracks and crevices
like some blobthing from a horror movie. Then it springs
overnight into a huge, seething green pit of slime that
covers the whole driveway to cause the Belching Beast
to slide into the neighbor's elegant border of St. John's
Wort. As you might imagine, this does little to enamor
me to my neighbors.

Maybe the reason most right-thinking humans
prefer lawns of grass to lawns of moss is that grass is
meek, and would never think of growing where it isn't
wanted.

To grass, you are God.

There is one place where moss grows where you
want it to grow: on the north side of trees. While this
is a significant aid to navigation, I have about as much
success growing trees where I want as I do growing
moss.

SPRING IN MY FACE

I woke up this morning, Spring was in my face. I
said, "Spring, get outta my face."

But Spring is here to stay. It arrived at 5:31 a.m. and
won't be leaving until June 21. I'm not certain of the
exact time Spring will get outta my face—but as far as
I am concerned, it can't be too soon. Spring means that
the grass will soon be growing. Otherwise intelligent

women will be at my favorite discount garden store, We B Green, scurrying through the aisles and fighting over little lawn statues of angels hugging lambs.

I suppose women like the fact that the sun warms the earth and flowers are blossoming everywhere. I suppose women enjoy the long, lazy evenings with the chianti sunsets over the mountains.

Humbug, I say. Spring sucks.

Once again, you will find women at We B Green, spending obscene amounts of money on stuff called turf enhancer and moss destroyer. Several hundred thousand dollars will be spent on lawn mowers, rototillers, weed slicers, hoses, rakes, sprinkler systems, dandelion poisons, seed planters, rhododendron feed, and a zillion other products.

Why? So men can't watch the NFL Europe or Arena Football.

Spring is probably the single biggest reason men can't watch football year round. Women all over the United States are rubbing their hands in glee, knowing full well that they will soon be able to say (if they haven't said it already), "Time to mow the lawn." These five words will be uttered minutes before kickoff. If you don't move fast, you'll probably get snared into killing moss or enhancing turf, too. You will be out in the yard because the woman in your life insists the grass is too long.

Here's a little-known fact, men: Grass that gets too long soon bends over of its own weight and looks as short as the stuff that is mowed. Not only that, but if you wait long enough, grass goes to seed and you can save yourself another football game if you let Mother Nature build your turf.

I have repeatedly expressed my dislike for Spring to B.B. Hardbody, yet like most women, she continues to hold to the romantic myth that men really like the season of renewal and are too stupid to know it. "Don't be silly," she says, "I know you like the sunshine. Here, take this sixty-gallon sprayer of weed killer and do the back forty before it rains."

Have you ever noticed that all the allergy advertisements feature sneezing women? Do you know why? Because women want you to think they are too allergic to mow the lawn, rebuild the turf, or do the back forty before it rains. Yes, I know that women "work" in the garden. You may actually see a woman planting bulbs, but how many women have you seen riding that 48-inch, 30-horsepower John Deere through the fescue?

Next winter can't arrive too soon. In the meantime, I'm fitting my mower with a portable TV.

SPRING FEVER

I'll bet you've got Spring Fever. You're probably just itching (maybe it's just pollen allergy) to get outside and mow your lawn.

I don't get Spring Fever, but I do get sick of spring. It always starts about the time Daylight Savings Time ends, without fail. First, I hear this droning, roaring sound. I don't hear it in the winter, except from the single true lawn-mowing Nazi zealot who lives down the block, who zip-cuts his turf every month of the year.

B.B. Hardbody suggested the other day that I might want to mow the lawn before leaving for a week-long snowsports journalists' conference in Bend, Oregon. The writers are real professionals and know how to hold a conference, with four days of skiing and maybe a lunch meeting thrown in for tax purposes.

Anyway, Hardbody thought the turf might grow so fast that it would be too thick and healthy to mow if it flourished for another week. It is for emergencies just such as this that I keep an empty gas can next to the old mower.

"You know I'd love to mow the turf," I told B.B., "but I'm out of gas."

"On the contrary," she says, "you are full of gas."

My theory is that mowing lawns is what gives people road rage. They whisk along on their green turf, chopping neat rows effortlessly through unobstructed back yards, then take their cars out on the highway. Here they encounter traffic jams and lights that always stay green twice as long for those geeks going in the opposite direction. It doesn't matter which direction they are traveling; the geeks going the other way get the long green. So they get so filled with road rage they beat each other senseless with Drive Friendly signs. They curse and wish they could just get back to mowing their lawn.

That's another reason I don't mow my lawn. I don't want to get road rage because with my luck, I'd be the only motorist brandishing a Drive Friendly sign when the cops showed up.

IV.   MALE BONDING

LUNKER CITY

My first visit to Lunker City and the annual Lake Conconully Male Bonding Ritual nearly turned into a disaster.

First, Grizzly Hemingway and Mr. Outdoors (not their real names) took a trip to Lunker City and very nearly to jail. Then Big Scribe offered to punch anybody's lights out if they tried to hug him. Big could do it, too. He is the only man I know who can pop the top off a quart bottle of beer by squeezing it.

Many people will tell you that male bonding and understanding maleness are merely means for certain counselors to make big bucks. We get in touch with our feelings while counselors get in touch with our wallets. But modern, sensitive men will tell you that there is much to be said for understanding your feelings. It was Little Scribe who said it best: "If I want to understand my feelings, I'll ask my wife."

Griz set the tone for the Male Bonding Ritual. "Let's go to Lunker City," he said. Griz is the only modern, sensitive man who can burp an entire sentence like that. Lunker City, he explained to Mr. Outdoors, is a secret lake that holds trout the size of Trident submarines. If you are going to understand your relationship with your father, Griz belched, you got to catch a lunker.

There were only two other anglers at Lunker City, camped in a trailer by the secret lake. Griz and Mr. Outdoors sped by to the boat launch. Mr. Outdoors had no more than guzzled his wake-up beer than Griz slammed his first huge trout on pink sparkly Power Bait and a treble hook. It peeled line so fast his reel smoked. "I think I already understand my father a little better," Griz belched.

He no sooner had landed the fish—at least three pounds—when Mr. Outdoors latched onto a four-pounder. The fish stirred Mr. Outdoors' primitive maledom so deeply he began to chant and dance while battling the fish.

"Whatsat yer singin?" Griz wanted to know.

"Gottagotobathroom, gottagotobathroom," chanted Mr. O.

The trout was so big that he had to fold it to fit into the cooler. Then he ran for the outhouse. There was a sign on the door. **"Selective Fishery,"** it said. **"See Page 6 in your Department of Fish and Wildlife Pamphlet."**

Mr. Outdoors was chanting another male-bonding tune when he returned to find Griz had ripped into two more mondo trout:

"Gointojailforsure, gointojailforsure."

When the trout thrashed in the cooler, it hopped along the ground. Mr. Outdoors had to sit on it while Griz consulted with one of the anglers camped in the trailer.

"Yeah," said the angler, "they ruined fishin' here.

One-fish limit. No bait. Barbless hooks.

"Say, what you guys got in that cooler?"

"Just a mess o' beer. Cooler's jumpin' like that 'cause beer has got hops in it." Griz cackled and belched at the same time, a horrible sound.

Then Mr. Outdoors and Griz decided they could understand their relationships with their fathers elsewhere. They grabbed their hopping, highly illegal catch and got the hell out of there.

MEET THE GANG

I recently returned from the annual Lake Conconully Male Bonding Ritual and thought it was about time I bored you with an account of all that took place.

First, you need to know the names of all the bondees. Grizzly Hemingway is a fly fisher; and then there's the Scotch Hippie, who makes chili that would melt a Spanish tile; and Lothario Mudmire, a birdwatcher who brings—for want of a more accurate term—culture to our group.

The bondees also include Big and Little Scribe. Big Scribe is our spiritual leader and the chief drummer during the bonding ritual. He usually drums on one of the other bondee's heads. Despite warnings to the contrary, Little Scribe eats Power Nuggets. "Tastes just like Puss 'n' Boots cat food," he says. None of us wants to know how he discovered that fact. Finally, there's me, Mr. Outdoors.

The original male-bonding ceremony was held

nearly three decades ago as several of the participants celebrated getting stuck in Spokane, Washington, when Mount St. Helens blew her top. I know, I know—many of you will say that getting stuck in Spokane is nothing to celebrate. Anyway, the years have added nothing but fine tradition to our gathering. We eschew typical male bonding practices, such as dancing, singing, and hugging. This is largely because Big Scribe promises that if anyone dances, sings, or hugs with him, he will rearrange their teeth with his fist.

This is no idle threat, either, since Big is about twelve feet tall. At the same time, it is a much more idle threat than it was three decades ago, because many of us no longer have our own teeth.

Another thing we avoid at our male bonding ritual is an emphasis on competition. As you know, competition is brought on by an overabundance of testosterone. Avoiding competition is especially difficult for Little Scribe because—I believe but cannot prove—Power Nuggets are loaded with testosterone.

So when Griz says, "First guy to catch a trout gets free beer the rest of the weekend," everyone ignores him. That is partly because the Scotch Hippie and Lothario Mudmire refuse to fish and partly due to the fact that Big has promised to rearrange our teeth if anyone catches a fish before him. Fishing was next to impossible at the lake, because the water was lower than a slug's belly in a dry creek bed. To get to the lake, you had to wade through a couple miles of mudflats.

The trout were so dry the best way to catch them was to flash a bucket of water in their direction, and they would jump out of the mud and into the bucket. Big caught a huge rainbow in this fashion and demonstrated his version of catch-and-release: catch the trout and release it into a big pan with bacon grease and cornmeal.

Some male bonding rituals simply can't be ignored.

THE HIPPIE SPEAKS

It was an unusually subdued ritual I attended at the Lake Conconully Male Bonding Trout Lip Rip and Beer Swill. There was no drumming to speak of, unless you count the Big Scribe's banging on the bar at the Sit 'N' Bull, or Little Scribe's thumping at the pool table.

Perhaps the biggest downer the whole weekend was the sad lack of wily trout. Lake Conconully is usually filled with wily trout, which are fed pellets that look suspiciously like lime green Power Bait with sparkles. These wily trout are dumber than a fire hydrant and twice as hungry. When you open up a jar of Power Bait, they jump into the boat. But vandals destroyed the hatchery and all of the stupid wily trout were lost. That left only the trout who survived from last year's planting in the lake, which meant there actually were wily trout swimming around. When you can avoid being caught in Lake Conconully for a whole year while six million anglers do everything including dropping depth charges on you from above, you are a survivor.

Obviously, the trout were a whole lot smarter than we were, because we didn't catch a thing—unless you count the bass I caught. Trout anglers are likely sneering or guffawing loudly at this minute, since to a trout angler, bass fishing is a step below buying fish at a supermarket. Grizzly Hemingway, who was with me when I battled the furious bucketmouth (that's angler talk for a largemouth bass) to the shore, even made up a tasteless joke about a bass angler:

This young man comes home from college and tells his father he has some upsetting news, news that could cause the family real heartache. "Well, son, what is it?" asks the father.

"I'm gay," says the kid.

The relief all over his father's face tells the whole story. "Gosh, son, I thought you were going to tell me you were a bass fisher."

Readers who fish for bass may feel free to substitute "trout angler" in the punchline. Gays may substitute "straight." Those who fish for salmon can substitute "bottomfisher," and so on.

The Scotch Hippie made his usual batch of Tex-Mex chili, which is often used in the cleansing ritual part of our male bonding weekend. It was hot enough to fuel a moon rocket and gave me enough gas to asphyxiate Chicago. Men who complain about not being able to get in touch with their feelings have never tried the Scotch Hippie's chili.

As has become tradition, our male bonding ceremonies avoid ridiculous and meaningless competition. We reject competition as a product of an insensitive, male-dominated society, one which thankfully appears to be obsolete. In fact, those very words are printed on the trophy we give to the bondee who can burp the alphabet backwards without passing out. Griz reached the letter "H" this year before falling onto the deck, unconscious as a bag of fertilizer. One of us took a photo to prove it.

Perhaps another reason our annual gathering lacked its usual spirit was because Lothario Mudmire was off teaching college. He refused to call in sick from Lake Conconully, as most of the rest of us do. So it was a small crowd. Big Scribe did not threaten to punch anyone's lights out; Little Scribe forgot to bring the instructions for building our sweat lodge; Griz and I exhausted ourselves flailing the lake into a white froth after the wily trout; and the Scotch Hippie took one bite of his Tex-Mex chili and was rendered senseless for the rest of the weekend.

Actually, the Hippie is such a quiet and unflappable guy that it is difficult to tell if he has been rendered senseless or just has nothing to say. It will be difficult when he dies—as we all must—to be certain he has done so.

The hit of the weekend was Little Scribe's home brew. Some people might imagine that our male bonding weekend is little more than an excuse to drink hundreds of gallons of beer, cuss and spit, and talk about women. Actually, ours is a cultured gathering and we appreciate beer merely for its taste. Griz is an expert brewmeister and Little Scribe, though a beginner, brought two quite different ales for our sampling.

"That one has a hoppy aftertaste," said Big Scribe, expertly tossing the empty bottle into the recycling bin across the lake.

"You're not supposed to taste the whole bottle in one

swallow," said Little. "Especially those quart bottles."

Our topic for the Feeling Fire this year was "male-bashing." The Feeling Fire is a big campfire we build on the beach. We write down our deepest feelings on pieces of kindling and then recite what we have written on them as we throw them into the fire. It helps men—who often refuse to admit they have them—talk about their feelings.

"Male-bashing sucks," said Hemingway, before throwing his stick into the fire. We all grunted agreement.

Little Scribe said he thought advertisements featuring really stupid men also suck, and we all agreed. Big Scribe said he didn't much like any of the male-bashing jokes that are going around these days, and again, we agreed.

I wrote, "Why must the sexes battle?" and everybody said that was profound.

Then it was the Scotch Hippie's turn. He stepped up to the Feeling Fire with his stick, paused to reflect a moment, then tossed it into the crackling blaze.

"Hmmmm," he said.

We weren't sure what he meant by that. But we were certainly happy to see that he was still alive.

GOOD BONDING, BAD FISHING

My friend Grizzly Hemingway (not his real name) and me (my real name) just returned from our annual male bonding ritual and fishing trip to Lake Conconully (its real name).

The bonding was good, but the fishing was less than perfect. You had to wade through several hundred yards of mud to get to the lake. Once there, we were rewarded with hatchery trout that would gladly take a bare hook. This is not entirely a bad thing, since it rebuilds my ego—shattered by attempting to fish with a fly.

Before we went meat-fishing (though a seven-inch trout could hardly be called "meat,") we stopped at Lunker City (not its real name) and Lake Chopaka (its real name), where you are required to fish with barbless hooks and artificial lures.

"I've long admired fly fishers like you," I told Griz. "You make it look so easy."

"It is easy," said Griz, fumbling with his float tube. "You just got to practice more. Learn how to fish with a barbless hook."

"That's the easiest part for me. I can get it out of my ear so much easier."

Lake Chopaka is an Okanogan lake regarded as one of the best fly fishing lakes in the state. You get there by driving up the Chopaka Grade outside of Loomis, Washington. Most anglers walk home, because their trucks and autos have been totally destroyed by the washboard road on the way up. If you can imagine being tied to an operating jackhammer for a month, you can get some idea of what it is like to drive the Chopaka

Grade. We were shaking so violently that Griz created a standing wave when he waded with his float tube into the lake, capsizing three float tubes and a steelhead boat.

The steelhead boat would have survived, but it was missing half its rivets from riding the road to the lake. Its trailer was demolished and lay with a huge pile of wrecked camp trailers, motor homes, truck springs, and one cracked Ford engine block.

I chose not to fish at Chopaka, largely because I did not want to be laughed off the water by anglers who could actually catch something other than their ear and cast farther than the tip of their rod. Griz thought this was silly and insisted that fly anglers were kind and understanding folk who, at one time or another, were as inexperienced as me. "Course, none of them had been practicing like you for the last half-century," he said. Then he cackled, making a sound just like my truck made before the engine fell out on the Chopaka Grade.

Griz not only fished at Chopaka. He caught and released at Chopaka. It was a trout that would barely fit in the Chevy shortbed pickup we found dead at the top of the Chopaka Grade. We spotted a small rattlesnake on the road on the way back to our camp at Lunker City. I briefly considered letting it bite my truck, simply to put it out of its misery.

OLD GUYS

I went to a gathering of old guys a few weeks back. It was pathetic.

In the first place, we used to be young guys. We got together once every year to bitch and moan about our jobs. We were young guys, bitching about our stupid bosses and moaning about how, if they only recognized our talent, we would be the bosses. I talked it over with B.B. Hardbody, and she pretty much agreed young women bitched and moaned about their stupid bosses, too.

But as old guys, we don't talk about our stupid bosses. We don't moan about how we could do it better. I believe this has less to do with the fact that bosses have gotten smarter and more to do with the fact that none of us can remember the stupid things bosses do from one minute to the next. Talk about geriatric: We only play poker for five minutes before one or another of us falls asleep. This phenomenon can occur without warning—Lothario Mudmire, who held the winning hand in the first deal, nodded off.

We were playing one-eyed-jacks, kings-stabbing-themselves-in-the-head-with-swords, twos, fours, and sixes wild (if you get a nine, you get an extra card), and Lothario started snoring like an asthmatic whale. He got a nine and held six aces, the highest hand you can get in Slam Dunk, the game we were playing.

Instead of swilling copious amounts of beer, like we used to do in the olden days, we sip tea that is supposed to sharpen your memory. We gobble prescription medicine for high blood pressure, depression, gout, low metabolism, bipolar symptoms, erectile dysfunction, prostate problems, and at least thirty-five other known old-guy disorders. This is how bad it has gotten:

I get out of the Bigfoot camper to greet Grizzly Hemingway, our host. "Griz! Good to see you, man! God, it's been a long time!"

"You came over last night. Got a new pair of jeans, heh?" asks Griz.

"How'd you know?"

Hemingway reaches down on my leg and pulls off the sizing tag. (Which, incidentally, is exactly the same waist size as I had when I was twenty years younger. Thank God for wide leather belts that don't break when you suck Stummick in and reef on them.). Now, it doesn't particularly bother me that I forgot to remove the sizing label. What bothers me is the fact that I wore the same jeans to a book signing and not a single one of the three people who showed up mentioned my sizing tag.

My greatest fear is that in five years, I will forget I've wet my pants. Nobody will tell me and I'll go grocery shopping, wandering the aisles with a gross, wet stain below my wide leather belt.

A couple of the regular guys couldn't make it to the reunion. The Little Scribe had planned to be there, but at the last minute decided it might be more prudent to stay at home to help his wife paint the kitchen. I think Big Scribe—who planned to take the Greyhound 300 miles to the reunion—got on the wrong bus and spent the weekend in Reno. That would suit Big nicely, because he loves to gamble. At our last reunion, he almost won $2,500 betting the Preakness. But he forgot the number of the horse he wanted to bet while walking to the window.

We're all excited about getting together next year. I told Hardbody I hoped I could remember the date.

"Maybe you'd better write it down, before you forget," she said.

"Write what down before I forget?"

She just mumbled something unintelligible and went back to reading her book.

V. ME AND STUMMICK

MY NEW COMPANION

I met a new companion over the holidays. I call my new companion Stummick.

Stummick and I met shortly after Thanksgiving dinner. One minute I was alone; the next, Stummick was there, keeping me company.

"Where did you come from?" I asked.

"I've always been here," Stummick growled. "You've just never noticed me before."

Ever since then, Stummick and I have been inseparable. Stummick watches the Seahawks with me, and seems to suffer with each loss as much as me. We sit there in our La-Z-Boy, slurping beer like it was lemonade on a hot summer day. We gobble nachos and Buffalo wings and boo the referee, even when Instant Replay makes it obvious to the both of us that the Seahawks are cheating.

I took Stummick with me and B.B. Hardbody to Big White Winter Resort in British Columbia for New Year's. Skip the Scott and Sharon the Strong met us at Big White. It was obvious from the very beginning that Stummick, Skip, and Sharon were not going to get along.

"Let's go skiing," said Skip and Sharon.

"Sounds like a great idea to me," I said.

"It looks awfully icy to me," Stummick growled. Stummick is always growling, and frankly, I wish he would just go away.

"Why don't we just sit here and have another beer?" he asked. "I think the Syrup of Ipecac Barf Bowl is on the tube; we need to watch it."

They had two great hot tubs at Big White, and I wanted in the worst way to soak my cares away. But I was embarrassed to take my new companion anywhere in public; he seems such a crass and vulgar fellow. B. B. Hardbody isn't fond of Stummick either. She says he's a big liar.

For example, I weighed myself just before New Year's. The scales said I weighed 186 pounds. Stummick said that didn't sound so bad. "Shoot, that's only about 11 pounds more than you used to weigh," he said. Then Hardbody told me the scales were 14 pounds off. I weighed 25 pounds more than I weighed before Stummick showed up.

Yeah, I'd like to get rid of Stummick. He's just a big white ugly thing that seems to hang around. In fact, there is just about only one good, positive thing I can say about Stummick. Since one of my New Year's resolutions is to say only good, positive things, this is it:

Stummick has given me a new appreciation for—and empathy with—pregnant women. I know there is a big difference, of course. For example, it only takes a few hours of pain to deliver a baby. But it's going to take me at least nine months of labor to get rid of Stummick.

WATCHING AND WORKING OUT

I was lounging in my La-Z-Boy the other day, swilling a beverage made from hops and artesian waters that originated in what was once a useless wetland—but is now a terrific golf course.

(Linksters wander hither and yon, chasing their little balls this way and that, unaware that this manicured brome once nourished thousands of wildland creatures. Ah, but today, birdies have replaced birds.)

Anyway, I was lounging and swilling and feeling downright guilty about both. It was a perfect day and the Great Outdoors beckoned like some siren's song wafting on the summer wind. Normally, I would have leaped from my La-Z-Boy and hit the trail, dragging B.B. Hardbody and Tar, the Wunderhund, along. But these are no longer normal times: NFL football season has arrived.

I could lounge in my La-Z-Boy, swilling beverage. I could curse the Seahawks and wonder if, maybe in the next twenty years, they'd win another game. When NFL season arrives, I gain more yards around my waist than the Seahawks gain the entire season. Much of this is due to the fact that by the end of their first pre-season game, I am so full of beverage that I could not get out of my La-Z-Boy even if I tried. But this year is going to be different—not about the Seahawks finally winning a game—but about my waist. This year, I'm going to follow the NFL Watch 'n' Workout Program.

The NFL Watch 'n' Workout Program was developed by Dr. Dirk Merkin, once sports-medicine physician to the Manchester Maulers PeeWee taxi squad. It provides a means whereby you watch NFL football, swill beverage, AND STILL GET A WORKOUT!

There's not enough room here to describe the entire regimen. You can read all about it at Dr. Merkin's Web site: www.sendmeyourmoney/beforeyoufigureout/thisisascam.com

It takes weeks—if ever—before Dr. Merkin sends you the NFL Watch 'n' Workout Program. In the meantime, here are two basic exercises:

The Beer Curl

This is easy to learn. Grab your favorite brewski and lift it to your mouth. Now switch hands and do it again. For the Beer Curl to be truly effective, you must exercise using a full beverage container every repetition. That means you must swill an entire can (bottles break and are not allowed in the gym!) with each rep.

Done properly, the Beer Curl gives you an added workout benefit. It greatly increases the number of times you must get up from your La-Z-Boy and walk to the bathroom.

The Pass the Chips

You'll need a spotter and a weighted container full of potato chips for this. Run across the room, hurdle the couch, and catch the container thrown by your spotter before it smashes the window.

I can personally vouch that I lost at least three pounds with this exercise alone. I dropped Hardbody's pass and had to run six miles before she stopped chasing me, brandishing her Alaska Native Ulu all the while.

WAISTING AN HOUR

OK, Stummick, this is the day I start getting rid of you. You've hung around long enough and all you do is eat, drink beer, and watch football.

Well, it all ends today. Right here on Green Mountain Road. What matters is this next sixty minutes, the first hour of the rest of my life.

Hmmm . . . if I die of exhaustion or drown in my own sweat in the next half hour of the rest of my life—what happens to the remaining thirty minutes? Is it credited to my next life?

Not that I believe in reincarnation. I don't even know if I believe in carnation. If there is reincarnation, I'd like to come back as an Olympic Raven. Sure wouldn't have to strap this twenty-five-pound pack on my back and hike up the Green Mountain Road to get rid of Stummick.

No sense wasting time. Now I've only got fifty minutes of the rest of my life to get rid of Stummick.

Hey, I never noticed that before. There are two slots cut in the tongue of my running shoes. I wonder what they're for? OK, I see, you're supposed to thread the shoelace through the slot to prevent the tongue from slipping down. Why the hell do I call these my "running shoes?" I couldn't run fifty feet in them without stroking out. I should call them waddling shoes. My very own pair of Asics Gel waddling shoes.

You dolt! You don't have to pull the laces all the way out to thread them through the tongue-holding-up slots. I wonder if these slots have a name, like tongueholds. That's what I'd call them if I were Mr. or Mrs. or Ms. Asics.

Hey, look at that: Somebody dumped garbage under that tree. I wonder if you could find out who did it by sifting through the junk for a label but then I suppose the label could be from just about anyone and not necessarily the geek who dumped the garbage there and what if I started messing around in the garbage and found a human hand or something equally repulsive and then I'd have to call the sheriff's deputies and report it and by God I'd never get started on the next hour of the rest of my life, which by the way, has been reduced by 38 minutes because I've been fumbling around with these stupid tongueholds.

Oh, great. Here come two women on mountain bikes. I suppose they'll think I'm some sort of pervert like those guys on the Channel 5 news who never register their perversions at the nearest law enforcement agency. Maybe they'll think I'm the pervert who put that hand in the garbage. I'll just wait in the car until they go by. Who knows what they'd think if I jumped out in my smelly sweats and started waddling up the road?

Besides, how can I get rid of Stummick in the first 10 minutes of the rest of my life? Maybe I'll start the first hour of the rest of my life tomorrow.

PLOTTING MURDER

"I suspect you're going to try to kill me again," said Stummick, my inseparable companion. "It is the New Year, after all, and we both know about all those resolutions everyone makes and breaks."

I have to admit: The thought of killing Stummick has crossed my mind. I haven't figured out exactly how I'm going to do it, though.

Some years ago I tried to murder Stummick by using the Nordic Track. It very nearly worked, too, until I slipped off the stupid Track and sprained my ankle. By the time my ankle healed enough to get back on Track, Stummick was hanging out with me again.

Then I tried to kill Stummick by making him walk four miles up Green Mountain with me every morning while I was wearing a twenty-five-pound pack on my back. This worked fine most of the summer, but it got very dark in the winter and I discovered it is much too easy to walk into a tree when you can't see where you are going.

We—B.B. Hardbody, Stummick, and I—went cross-country skiing the other day. I would have been happy to leave Stummick behind, but my behind is already big enough. The fact that my behind is already big enough does not bother me, especially when I am cross-country skiing. See, you can't fall as far or as hard if you have a big behind.

From time to time when I am cross-country skiing, I try to fall on Stummick, hoping maybe to crush him. Certainly having a weighty behind would help in this regard, but more often than not, my head lands in the snow before Stummick. There's a good side and a bad side to cross-country skiing with Stummick. The good side is that you can go downhill faster and people are much more likely to get out of your way. The bad side, I have discovered, is that every downhill trail I take is uphill on the way back.

Anyway, I've been thinking of some other ways to get rid of Stummick this year. I'm certain that whatever method I choose will involve substantial amounts of both sweat and pain. Those are two things that are universal to any New Year's resolution. People never make New Year's resolutions that involve comfort or pleasure. What person in the proper frame of mind, for example, would resolve to eat more chocolate? Have you ever resolved—or known anyone to resolve—to sleep in more often?

The reason we make resolutions that involve sweat and pain is because those two things make it much easier to break our resolutions. Resolutions, like promises, are made to be broken.

Perhaps this year, I'll resolve to make Stummick my friend. I'll buy him dinner every night and bake marvelous desserts for him. There will be no sweat or pain involved and for the first time in my life, I'll make a New Year's resolution I can actually keep for more than two weeks.

THE FREEZE-DRIED DIET

I was hoping to lose my vulgar and constant companion, Stummick, while backpacking in the mountains. But Stummick just hung out, growling about how much work I was making him do.

I have tried increasingly desperate measures to get rid of Stummick. I have even attempted more exercise, but all that seems to do is increase my appetite and thirst. Stummick appears to thrive on this solution. I am at my wit's end—not to mention my end's end, which seems to be growing proportionately with Stummick.

My most recent attempt to lose Stummick appeared promising, at least on paper. I would go deep into the woods, huffing and wheezing like an asthmatic wild boar, and not eat anything but freeze-dried food for a whole week. Those of you who have eaten freeze-dried food understand how this causes a sudden and catastrophic effect on your digestive system. Those of you who have not tried freeze-dried food can understand by trying the following recipe:

1. Take equal parts of Metamucil and Presto-Log and place in a blender or food processor.
2. Add one cup of boiling water.
3. Process or blend for one minute.
4. Place in a plastic bag and eat with a big camp spoon (reserve the plastic bag, just in case).

Perhaps now, one and all can see how you might lose weight in the wilderness. I might have done so, except that after five days, even freeze-dried food begins to taste good. So I have gone to more extreme measures to rid myself of Stummick. I have tried the Atkins Diet, which turns out to be my kind of diet.

I used to worry about fat, but Dr. Atkins says I don't need to worry about fat. I like this because I love bacon, and we all know that bacon has a whole mess of fat. Never mind that your blood flows through your veins like library paste. Now I enjoy a rasher of bacon for breakfast, two or three slices (with tomato and cheese) for lunch, and a pound or two of thick-sliced for dinner. B.B. Hardbody says it is me who is the pig, not the bacon.

Hardbody says I am a "Jack" Atkins dieter. By that she means I only follow the part of the diet that appeals to me. For example, Dr. Atkins says you should stop drinking alcohol and real coffee, but I would sooner eat freeze-dried food for a whole year. Worse, Dr. Atkins says you can't eat any carbohydrates for two weeks. Chocolate has carbohydrates. So does everything else in the universe that tastes good.

Stummick appears to think the jury is still out on the Atkins Diet. This may be due to the fact that the first thing you notice on the diet is a certain restriction in the normal ebb and flow of the digestive process.

I solved this minor problem by downing equal parts of Metamucil and Presto-Log. Stummick complained about it, but I gave him no choice in the matter.

MY SKI PAL

I took Stummick on a ski trip to New Mexico. I would much rather have had the company of B.B. Hardbody, but she had to do legitimate work and besides, I don't think she likes Stummick very much.

Stummick is not too fond of her, either. In fact, I'm not certain Stummick likes anybody or anything—except eating. Eating is pretty much all my companion did in New Mexico. I went skiing at Taos while Stummick ate. Then I went skiing at Red River Canyon and Stummick ate. Then Stummick ate while I skied at Angel Fire.

"I'm going skiing," I'd say to my constant companion. "How about you?"

"I'll just hang out," said Stummick. Stummick pretty much hung out the whole trip.

The skiing was great, although there wasn't much snow. But it is tough to complain about a lack of snow when the sun shines and turns the mountains into ragged rubies every evening. Compensating for the paucity of snow was the overabundance of good food. Stummick flourished, I am ashamed to tell you. In the first place, they eat chili in New Mexico. It is a different sort of chili than you can find around here, and people eat it with everything. You can eat chili with eggs, or chili with peanut butter and jelly, or chili with ice cream. They have red chili and they have green chili. Stummick was fond of mixing the two colors together, although I was told the residents of New Mexico only do that at Christmas.

One of Stummick's favorites was a dish called "Frito Pie." To call it a dish is not entirely accurate, because the authentic Frito Pie is served in a bag.

Here is the recipe for Frito Pie:

One small bag of Fritos

One big ladle of Texas chili

Chopped onion, jalapeno, shredded cheese, lettuce, guacamole, and crushed Tums (The Tums are my own custom addition to this traditional recipe.).

To prepare:

Open the bag of Fritos. Dump the Texas chili into the bag and cover with the onion, jalapeno,

shredded cheese, lettuce, and guacamole. Garnish with crushed Tums to taste.

Enjoy!

Not all of the food was so plebeian. In fact, Stummick confided to me that he hadn't eaten such *haute cuisine* in years—and not simply because we were 9,500 feet *haute* in Taos.

For example, I decided to eat light at the Trading Post, a splendid restaurant in Taos. So I ordered the *carpaccio* and a simple spinach salad. But Stummick would have none of it, and insisted on the duck. I practically had to drag my companion out of there. Then one of our hosts served a delicious seven-course meal that included a *pate* of *foie gras* and poached salmon in a morel sauce. It was enough good food for the entire village, but Stummick growled about not getting two puff pastries for dessert.

One morning, I ate breakfast at a wonderful European inn at Taos Ski Valley. I thought a simple bowl of cereal with fruit would be nice, but Stummick insisted on the fritatta with gorgonzola and sausage patties (and, of course, green chili). He is such a vulgar companion. On another evening, we drank splendid champagne and velvety *pinot noir.* Stummick made a real pig of himself at the table, gobbling such items as a *terrine* of smoked scallops and black mussels, white truffle *gnocchi* and a *confit* of duck over sundried tomato custard with a basil *beurre rouge*.

You have no idea how badly I wanted to leave Stummick in New Mexico, but my companion insisted on coming home with me. Frankly, Stummick was so gross I worried the plane might not get off the runway.

VI. HOLIDAYS

MY FIREWORKS TALE

I always wait until Independence Day has passed before I bore people into irrecoverable stupor with my fireworks story. I don't want anyone to accuse me—as I am certain they would—of encouraging our impressionable youth to play with fireworks. From the looks of the neighborhood after every July 4, they need no encouragement anyway. The place always looks like they just fought the Battle of Yorktown.

First, a **POP QUIZ:**

July 4, Independence Day, celebrates what event in American history?

A. The release of Patrick Henry from the stockade after he screamed, "Give me liberty or give me death!" at a fancy costume ball. (It is little known that Patrick Henry was a cross-dresser and thought nobody would recognize him in drag.)

B. The passage of the Bill of Rights.

C. The signing of the Declaration of Independence.

D. The signing of the Magna Carta.

If your answer was C, you may go to the head of the class. If you know the significance of the Magna Carta to American history, you can pass Go. And if you don't know what the Bill of Rights is, you can go directly to jail.

Now, the fireworks story:

It was just a few years after the signing of the Declaration of Independence when Dickie Dudelsack and I blew up Hayden and Spirit Lakes, Idaho. In the process, we launched the first American satellite, a garbage can, using multiple cherry bombs.

Dickie was a rich kid and at least as much of a pre-delinquent as me. Before we graduated from sixth grade, he brought a fireworks catalog to school. It wasn't that wimp "safe and sane" stuff, either. It was Real Man fireworks. There were cherry bombs, buzz bombs, TNT sticks—even a limited nuclear device. At least, it said "A-Bomb" on it.

Dickie wanted to split an assortment with me. He would have it mailed to the Hayden Lake Post Office and I could tell my parents he gave me my half. I mowed 3,612 lawns in May and June to earn $7.50, my half of the cost. For $15, we got the "World War II" assortment. There was enough gunpowder in it to level the Kingdome—if the Kingdome hadn't already been leveled years ago.

We started blowing up Hayden Lake immediately, at Dickie's two-day birthday party. Those of you who know Hayden Lake will be interested to know that Mokins Bay did not exist until July 4, 1953. Later I took my half of the loot to Spirit Lake, where my brother and I blew part of Mount Spokane into Brickle Creek, which created a land barrier and reversed its flow into the lake for three days. (The garbage can, incidentally, re-entered the earth's atmosphere over Mount Rainier, creating the very first flying saucer scare.)

Shortly thereafter, one of my brother's friends accidentally launched a buzz bomb in our house and stepped on it to prevent its flight. It blew a three-inch deep crater in our hardwood floors.

I was greatly relieved that it wasn't little Dickie Dudelsack, or any of my friends.

WORKING ON LABOR DAY

Have you ever wondered why nobody works on Labor Day? I have.

I don't suppose I blame anybody for not working on Labor Day, though. I certainly wouldn't work on Labor Day if I didn't have to. But since it is the last official day of camping season and I am, after all, Mr. Outdoors, I always work on Labor Day. I pack up B.B. Hardbody and Tar, the Wunderhund, in the Bigfoot camper and we go to work.

Actually, I am the only one who works. They just sit around, swilling Labor Day libations and telling lies about the big fish they caught or the long hike they took. They don't understand one another because Hardbody doesn't speak a word of French poodleese and of course Tar refuses to speak English. You're probably thinking that animals can't talk, but I'm pretty certain you'd change your mind if you heard a Brahma bull tell you to get off its back. Surely that is the message a herd of rodeo bull riders get.

Anyway, Hardbody and Tar don't work on Labor Day, but I do. It is hard work, too.

First, I've got to get us to the campground. This means at least two solid hours of cursing other drivers. That may not seem like hard work to you, but after two hours, I actually run out of curses and have to start repeating myself. I suppose it would be worse if I weren't driving close to five tons of machinery at a little more than a mile a minute. Labor Day drivers have a tendency to give slightly more respect to a huge truck and camper driven by a cursing fool than they might an elderly woman in a 1957 Dentmobile.

Then, once I get us to the campground, I have to work to get us a spot. This often proves to be the hardest work of all, since all of the spots are usually already taken. I enjoy this work most of all, however, because it calls upon my highly developed creative intelligence. One of my favorite tactics, especially during a dry autumn, is to pull up to the campsite of my choice and confront the occupant. I'll swagger up to him and say:

"Excuse me, sir. I'm Warden Gluck from Fire District 18 and I'm afraid I've got some bad news. We've got some firefighters coming in tonight, haven't had a night's sleep in seventeen days. They just got off the fire line and well, we're just going to have to take your spot.

"There'll be a whole platoon of 'em coming in about an hour, and they're gonna have to evacuate the whole campground."

I do a mess of other work on Labor Day, too. After

all, it is every bit as hard driving home after Labor Day as it is getting to the campground, although having four-wheel drive sometimes helps.

The only thing that is easier about driving home is this: I don't have to find a campsite.

KEEPING YOUR RESOLVE

Several years ago, I made a New Year's resolution that I would never break any of my resolutions. I am extremely proud to say that I have faithfully stuck to every resolution I have since made.

For example, four years ago, I resolved to eat more sweets. It was tough to stick to, as you might imagine, but I have managed to eat increasingly more sweets every year. If you don't believe me, you can ask Stummick. I resolved to gain at least five pounds over the course of one year, as well. I suppose that goes hand in hand with eating more sweets, but you can see that sticking to this resolution was a good deal easier than resolving to lose five pounds over the course of a year.

Where some folks might resolve to drink less beer, I have promised myself to drink more. I also made every effort to watch more football this year than I did last. That was a real challenge, since I am certain that with my satellite TV, I only missed one professional and two college games last year.

A friend has declared the month of January to be "Your Body is Your Temple Month." She and her husband resolve not to eat or drink anything harmful during the month, which of course cuts out 99 percent of the food and drink worth consuming. That's the kind of resolution that can get you in big trouble, not to mention lowering your self-esteem when you give in to that last slice of raspberry-chocolate cheesecake. I have no such self-esteem problems, largely because I have no esteem for myself.

The only resolution I have had difficulties with so far is the promise I made to myself to make at least three backcountry ski camping trips every winter. "I want to get back in touch with snow, to sleep on the bare white bosom of winter, to float through mountains of white fluff," I told B.B. Hardbody.

"You need to get back in touch, for sure. With reality," said Hardbody.

See, she has slept on the bare white bosom of winter. She knows it is about as comfortable as grabbing a little shuteye in a bathtub full of frozen margaritas. The only advantage to the margaritas is that after three or four gulps, you don't care if you are freezing to death.

Anyway, I had problems with that resolution. I was supposed to make my first winter camping trip recently. I planned a four-day excursion to the Olympic Mountains. I figured I could hike up there in one day. I'd mess up the smooth white slopes with large craters from my falling body for two days, then ski home on the fourth day.

But I realized I'd miss the Super Bowl. And I resolved this year to watch more football this year than last. As I mentioned, I intend to keep all my resolutions from now on.

Well, most of them, anyway.

THE PSYCHIC GIFT HOTLINE

I called the Psychic Hotline the other day in a desperate attempt to find out what I should give B.B. Hardbody for Christmas.

"This is Madame Zrbinga," said a woman. "How may I help you?"

"You're a psychic?" I asked. "I thought you would know."

Well, it turns out that Madame Zrbinga did give me a few ideas for Christmas gifts. But it was only after we established through extensive questioning that I was not pregnant, cheating, or trying to get spiritual help in finding my lost car keys. Down in Los Angeles, they have psychic gift counselors, which I think is a terrific idea. For your firstborn and a couple thousand dollars, they will tell you what anyone wants for Christmas.

"I was hoping you could tell me what Hardbody wants for Christmas," I said.

"Hardbody. Hmm. He wants a set of Craftsman tools. An air compressor. A case of Budweiser."

"Hardbody is a woman. I call her that because she is stronger than the Hulk and the Destroyer, combined."

"I knew that. I knew that," said Madame Zrbinga. "I was talking to Butch on another wavelength. Hardbody wants a platinum-set diamond. A case of perfume. A quiet evening beside the fire in a Sun Valley condo."

"So is there anything she wants that I can afford?"

"Not after this phone call, buddy. We got your credit card number," said Madame Zrbinga. She cackled like a seagull choking on a clam.

That Madame Zrbinga has my credit card number

does not worry me greatly, because I can transfer balances faster than you can say "Mele Kalikimaka," which is Hawaiian for "Humbug." It would take Madame Zrbinga at least two years to trace my Visa Rubbercard through the seventy-two banks, twelve oil companies, and at least two phone companies before discovering my account has been closed since Halloween.

It is always so difficult for me to figure out what to give a person for Christmas. I know, I know: It is the thought that counts.

Those of you who are having trouble thinking of the right gift for a friend should try this: Wrap up an empty box all pretty with red and green bows and silvery paper. Put a snowflake card on it that says, "For my Friend."

"What's this?" your friend will ask when he or she opens the box.

"A thought. I hope you like it."

Your friend will undoubtedly grab the case of Budweiser or perfume he or she just gave you and catch the next sleigh out of town. You can save your thought for next Christmas. You've heard it before, and you will hear it again: Christmas has become too materialistic. It is the spirit of giving that counts, not the gift. That is why I always ask Santa for small gifts. The tiniest diamond. Just a little bitty oil well. A two-person Learjet instead of a Boeing 747.

As for Hardbody, I'm headed to the mall in one final hopeless attempt to find just the right gift. Madame Zrbinga predicted they would be out of platinum by now.

MEMORIAL DAY CAMPING

I don't know why, but I'm going to remember this Memorial Day. There's just something about the long Memorial Day weekend that makes you want to remember stuff.

Like, I remember last Memorial Day, when I spent the weekend camping with B.B. Hardbody and Tar, the Wunderhund. We camped in a parking lot, which was not the only space available, but the only space where I could get a clear shot at a satellite to watch the Indy 500.

That's roughing it.

Memorial Day camping these days is tough. First, you must fight traffic so heavy that if you get to your campsite before the weekend is over, you are doing very well indeed. Most people these days just turn around when they get there and start fighting the same traffic to get home. Today, we've not only got to fight the traffic, but we fight road rage. I don't understand road rage. I never get mad at the stinking fools who cut in front of me and slam on their brakes then speed ahead only to slam on their brakes again before they cut in front of somebody else and slam on their brakes so that driver gets mad at them and chases them and they're weaving in and out of traffic and cutting everyone off and then one of the slimy bastards rams into the other's car and smashes his face into the windshield and beats him about the head and face with a tire iron and renders him senseless and there's blood all over and by God, the little puke deserves it and you can take that to the bank, Bucko.

No. I'm calm and always in control.

I have heard, but find it difficult to believe, that some people don't go camping on Memorial Day. There certainly can't be a lot of them, because I am certain I have seen everyone in the United States at my secret camping spot on Memorial Day. My secret Memorial Day camping spot is located somewhere in the national forest. Of course, I can't tell you where it is exactly, because then it would not be a secret. I suppose you could just follow everyone in the United States if you really wanted to find out where it is.

Most Memorial Day campers find their secret spots by trying to think of someplace nobody else has thought about. This is a big mistake, because everyone in the United States is trying to think of someplace nobody else has thought about, and they are all thinking of the same place about which you are thinking.

The trick is to think of someplace that everybody else thinks would be way too crowded, so they don't bother about going there. Your secret spot needs to be the place most people regard as the most crowded, vulgar camping site on earth. You'll be the only person there.

Just don't pick someplace like a cemetery. For some reason, a whole lot of people go there on Memorial Day, too.

FIREWORKS WARNING!

Watch your fingers. Here comes the Fourth of July.

July 4 warning No. 1: Children shouldn't play with fireworks. You adults should make certain to have all the fun.

Several years ago, I followed my own advice and nearly blew myself into another universe. Operating on the assumption that law enforcement officers were way too busy cruising someone else's neighborhood for illegal fireworks, I fired up a huge aerial bomb. I wish to report that while the aerial bomb had plenty of bomb to it, it had very little aerial. Perhaps the aerial part of the bomb referred to the explosion which pretty much blew me off the ground.

WARNING! WARNING WILL ROBINSON! FIREWORKS CAN BE HARMFUL TO YOUR HEALTH!

July 4 warning No. 2: Pets don't celebrate July 4, largely because no dogs, cats, alligators, or gerbils signed the Declaration of Independence after July 4, 1776, when it was adopted by the Second Continental Congress. Therefore pets should be kept inside, away from all the noise and hubbub and to keep them from eating more than their share of strawberry shortcake.

July 4 warning No. 3: Don't argue with your spouse about the origins of Independence Day. For instance, don't say something stupid like: "Everyone knows why we celebrate July 4 with fireworks. It symbolizes the rockets' red glare that Francis Scott Key wrote about in 'The Star Spangled Banner.' "

That is the stupid something I said to B.B. Hardbody a couple of years ago on July 4. She just cackled like a kid who breathed a whole helium balloon. **(DANGER! DANGER WILL ROBINSON! BREATHING HELIUM CAN BE HARMFUL TO YOUR HEALTH!)**

"You star-spangled twit," she said. "Francis Scott Key did not write 'The Star Spangled Banner' until the War of 1812. He copied the tune from an old British drinking song, 'To Anacreon in Heaven.' " Hardbody is full of little tidbits of valuable information like that. I often accuse her of being full of something else, but in the interests of keeping my body in one piece, seldom do so within her hearing range.

July 4 Warning No. 4: Never quote the Declaration of Independence by saying:

"Four score and seven years ago . . ."

or:

"We the people, in order to form a more perfect union . . ."

Those are from two other historic American documents that many of us have pretty much forgotten. The Declaration of Independence begins:

"When, in the course of human events . . ." And it mentions that we are endowed with inalienable rights, including "Life, Liberty and the pursuit of Happiness."

You may have guessed from the above that I am a dedicated student of American history. Indeed, I have studied the Declaration of Independence at great length and am certain that Thomas Jefferson's original version included a fourth inalienable right—to eat as much

98

chocolate as you want. This fourth right was removed when Congress reviewed Jefferson's document. You see, though rebellious, members of Congress were still partial to English toffee.

You have been warned.

GETTING AROUND

You've got to hand it to those guys in the Travel Industry Association of America. You might say they really get around.

They sent me a bunch of facts about travel and a bunch of facts about the Travel Industry Association of America. You might say they want you to really get around, too. That is because the travel industry is a $582 billion business and the association would like to make it even more. Very few of those dollars, I'm relieved to report, formerly belonged to me.

The reason for that is because I am cheap. B.B. Hardbody says that I would spend a quarter for gum, chew it into a wad, and put it on a stick, just to fish a dime out of a storm drain. I don't think I am that cheap, but I might do it for a buck. We travel by truck and camper, which is the cheapest way to go unless you count the fact that my truck gets around two gallons per mile when it is carrying the camper. On the very rare occasions I travel by air, I have noticed that all of the other passengers are traveling on business—or are planners, consultants, or emergency services coordinators, which means they are not paying for their tickets.

I believe I would travel by air a lot more if I could get someone to buy my ticket and pay for my food and lodging. But I have been unable to convince anyone that they should buy me a ticket to Disneyland so I can do research or attend a conference. Anyway, here are some facts from the Travel Industry Association of America:

—Two percent of 29 million travelers in the U.S. take their pet bird with them on trips. Three percent travel with a fish, rabbit, or ferret. Statistics for traveling turtles are not available.

—Florida is at the top of the ten most desirable vacation spots. Surprisingly, neither Pucker Huddle nor Humptulips, Washington made the list.

—Three-quarters of all summer trips will be taken in an auto, truck, or recreational vehicle. Twenty-two percent will be by airplane and 1.9 percent by bus, train, or bicycle. The remaining 0.1 percent of travelers will be walking on their hands.

Here are some frequently asked questions by travelers, according to the association:

—Are the Amish in season?

—What time does the nine o'clock ferry leave? (That is a legitimate question with some—I am not naming names—ferry systems.)

—How many miles of undiscovered cave are there?

—How come all of the war battles were fought in national parks?

—Does the bus tour go the same places that the boat tour does?

—Why don't you have more signs saying to keep

the area pristine?

—Are you expecting any earthquakes?

—And, a question I frequently ask myself: At what time of the year are the fewest Californians here? (Offended Californians are perfectly welcome to substitute Washingtonians or Oregonians, if they wish.)

ANTI-TOURISM

Dry, sunny weather is one of the biggest dangers of the summer. It causes conditions ideal for both forest fires and tourists.

Nobody wants forest fires, of course. What I find interesting is that there are some folks who don't want tourists, either. Such folks wander about our streets, searching for people who wear socks with sandals and loud Hawaiian shirts, assuming these people are tourists. These naysayers then accost the tourists, saying things like:

"Go away!"

And:

"Soon it's gonna rain, I can feel it."

And:

"Soon it's gonna rain, I can tell."

Sometimes they sing those last two quotes to a tune from "The Fantastiks." I think that does little to add to their message. As difficult as it may be for you to believe, a strong Anti-Tourist sentiment exists locally. It's not as bad as the sign we once saw during a distant community festival: "Go Home, Yuppie Scum," but it does show its ugly head around here from time to time.

When B.B. Hardbody and I were doing the tourist bit, I heard a local resident telling his out-of-state relatives, "Yep, this is probably the first day of the year we haven't had any rain. I saw a dehydrated slug in the driveway this morning." As nearly as I can tell, Anti-Tourists are trying to keep as many potential residents from deciding they really like it here. It seems a bit dishonest to me, but Anti-Tourists I know say they are simply giving a dose of reality to potential residents.

"You want a bunch of Californians to move in next to you," one A-T friend said, "it's on your head."

"What's on my head?"

"The hatred and resentment they'll feel toward you when it starts to rain and doesn't stop for six months. They should put a ban on tourists from July through August, same as they do a ban on fires.

"Why, we should have those same signs they use in the Forest Service, only instead of 'Fire Danger: High' it should say 'Tourist Danger: High.' "

I said I thought that was a bit extreme. Tourists are an excellent source of revenue, I argued. "Puma pellets," said my A-T friend, who was raised in the southwest, where they call cougars "pumas" simply because it would be too unrefined to say "cougar crap" even though it is equally alliterative.

"Tourists don't bring any new revenue to the local economy. They simply recirculate the money they rip off from us when we go wherever they live."

"I suppose," I said. "But it doesn't seem fair to keep

all this good weather to ourselves."

"Pika poop," said my acquaintance, "we're the ones who suffer through fifty weeks of slop for two weeks of sunshine. We paid our dues."

I said the same thing I always say when there is nothing more to say, a saying I learned from a famous journalist who is not so famous that I remember his name:

"You may be right."

THERE'S ONLY ONE CHRISTMAS

Here comes Peter Cottontail, hopping down the bunny trail.

Somebody—was it Gene Autry or Burl Ives?—was singing those very words about the time I figured out that Easter was good for almost as much candy as you could get around Christmas. I much preferred the Christmas candy to the Easter candy because it came prepackaged in a stocking.

At Easter, you actually had to get out there in the fescue, wet with morning dew, and wrestle with other kids for it. That was work.

My dad would always sneak off to the local candy store a couple of days before Easter and buy candy that looked exactly like fried eggs and bacon. He'd put it on a plate after we came inside from wrestling all those kids, but of course he wouldn't let us eat candy for breakfast. More often than not, we had to choke down a couple of the hard-boiled eggs Peter Cottontail had spilled out of his basket while he was hopping down the bunny trail. These would most often be served with something called a Hot Cross Bun, which at least provided some sugary reminder why we celebrate Easter in the first place.

I'm usually not one to ramble on about how I used to walk a mile to elementary school every day; about how tough I had it when I was a youngster compared to the wimps and weaklings we are raising today. But I will say this: I have witnessed catered dinners that are rougher than modern-day Easter egg hunts.

Here's little Junior and Missy, chortling and bouncing through the fescue, wet with dew, on a modern Easter egg hunt. No fewer than one step behind trails Mommy or Daddy—often both—making sure that Missy or Junior don't get grass stains on any of their Easter finery. "Look over there, honey," says Mommy or Daddy, "there's something Peter Cottontail left." I don't think a youngster could find an egg by himself today unless it had a pager.

Bunny droppings. You might as well just go out there with a basket and pick them up yourself.

Another thing—today you have to listen to all those warnings from the health department. Make sure your eggs are boiled for three days. And make sure the kids sterilize the eggs and candy before they eat them; after all, they've been sitting in that fescue for at least thirty minutes and you can never tell what kind of nasty critter sniffed at that egg after Peter Cottontail laid it.

And just what kind of myth is that, anyway? A bunny is a mammal, and mammals don't lay eggs. I didn't believe it as a kid and I frankly think it is as dangerous to let our youngsters believe mammals lay eggs as it is to follow along behind the little beggars, pointing out eggs they should be able to find for themselves. I mean, we are talking here about our future. Now is the time to instill in Junior and Missy something called the "survival instinct." Do you think they will develop the survival instinct if Mommy and Daddy are always there to point out the Easter eggs?

Of course not.

You want your kids to grow up with the will to survive, don't you? Then you'd better find them an old-fashioned Easter egg hunt, one where older kids armed with pea-shooters and squirt guns lurk in the bushes, waiting for your kid to bounce by, chortling. It's like tough love. You've got to show the kids that if they want something worthwhile, like Easter eggs, they've got to work for it.

Christmas, after all, comes only once a year.

MOTHER'S DAY

My mother's birthday always followed Mother's Day by one week. This was extremely fortunate for someone as cheap as me.

I could buy her a card for Mother's Day and still afford a birthday present for her. When I was young, a couple of centuries ago, I always seemed to find the perfect gift. One year, I got her a cap pistol that was so real it had bullets that you pulled apart to stick the caps inside. I got her a turtle once, but it died before her birthday, so I told her it was fertilizer for her roses.

She professed to love my gifts, which of course I generally enjoyed much more. Some time after she died, I was cleaning out some of her stuff and was surprised to find she had saved the cards I gave her.

Mom had a sense of humor and I have always felt that it was one of the great gifts she gave me. One of the funniest things to her—and to me today—are people who have no sense of humor.

Mom also taught me that authority and intelligence often don't mix. An FBI agent once came to our house to ask about a friend of mine who had registered as a conscientious objector.

"He says he doesn't want to go to war," the FBI agent told my mom.

"Does anyone?" Mom asked.

She was a fairly typical woman of the '50s, I suppose, although I naturally thought she was special. She spent a good portion of her day picking up after me and my brother, and we spent a good portion of our day thoughtfully leaving things for her to pick up. Once, after she had spent most of her day picking things up, an encyclopedia salesman came to the door. My mom answered the door and politely told him she wasn't interested.

He rang the doorbell a second time and my mom again was polite, but short. "I haven't time now. We're not interested," she said.

The doorbell rang a third time. Mom stopped picking up for the third time and answered the door. This time she left the storm door closed and shouted through it to the same salesman.

"Go pee up a rope," she said. Then she closed the door and went back to picking up after us.

She loved books and was always reading one thing or another. She had collected more than 5,000 books before she lost her sight to macular degeneration. I wanted to buy her talking books, but she said it wasn't the same as reading them for herself. She introduced me to books by Joseph Heller, Terry Southern, and Kurt Vonnegut Jr.

She came home alone, once, to find a stranger prowling our garage. She got out of the car and grabbed a rake and started waving it at him. "Get out of here right now!" she yelled. The stranger left, though not in a great enough hurry to suit my mom. She chased him down the block, waving the rake.

"Damn, I must have been crazy," she said later. "What if he had a gun? What was I going to do, rake him to death?"

That thought always amused her. I am thankful to her that it amuses me, even today.

THE BIG FAMILY

It has been years since we've done the tourist bit, so when Big—B.B. Hardbody's brother—paid us a visit recently, we did the tourist bit. Big brought his wife, Mrs. Big, and kids, Big Jr. and Bigette.

Big, Mrs. Big, Big Jr., and Bigette are not their real names. You may have already guessed that. Big really isn't much bigger than me and Mrs. Big is a petite woman, but they call them Big and Mrs. Big back home in Whitefish, Montana. We call them that because Big is the size of their hearts.

The tourist bit has changed since the last time I did it. Once upon a time, you could make a reservation for dinner at good restaurants. Today, you've got to have a party of thirty-six or more before you can reserve a table. I called one local restaurant to make a reservation and talked to Vinnie, the headwaiter. "You need a party of eight to reserve a table," he said. "If you don't show up, we charge your credit card for dinner anyway."

"No problemo," I lied, "there are eight in our party."

"Gimme a name," said Vinnie. At this point Big, who has an excellent sense of humor, suggested we tell Vinnie our name was Donner. When our table was ready, Vinnie would call out, "Donner, party of eight. Donner, party of eight."

And we would say, "That's us . . . but two of our party didn't make it." Big and Mrs. Big are much too refined to do so, but I proposed to belch at that point and perhaps pick my teeth.

We packed enough stuff into one week to keep a whole busload of Japanese tourists busy until 2008. We took a harbor tour. We went to the ocean. We went up in the Space Needle. I got airsick in the elevator and Hardbody refused to go anywhere in public with me. When we got to the ocean, they wanted to go swimming and wondered if they would be stung by jellyfish. I told them not to worry, I'd never seen a stinging jellyfish in the ocean, and I'd been there at least twice before. So they went swimming in the ocean and everyone but me got stung by a jellyfish. Big Jr. got stung worst.

I wouldn't blame Big Jr. if he never visited us again. The day after he got stung by the jellyfish, he got sick and barfed around various Seattle tourist traps.

I volunteered to drive the Big family car around Seattle. I could tell they did not feel comfortable in such heavy traffic, especially when they were stacking the SUVs three deep at that place where the Mariners play. I don't have any problem in heavy traffic, especially when I am driving somebody else's car with out-of-state license plates. Things went well until I knocked Big's mirror off trying to get out of an underground parking lot built for Tonka toys.

We got out of town shortly thereafter. Everyone seemed grateful that we won't do the tourist bit again for at least another year.

VII. THE GREAT OUTDOORS

WINTER CAMPING

It has been several years since I camped on snow in the middle of winter. As we are all wont to do, I have repressed all the miserable memories of winter camping and recall only the good ones.

The reason I haven't camped on snow lately is that I am reluctant to leave all the winter comforts of my Bigfoot camper for a two-person tent. The camper has a furnace, hot and cold running water, microwave, color TV with VCR. The tent only has a refrigerator, just outside the door. If I had been smart enough in the good old days to record my winter camping adventures, it would have helped me remember all the bad things that happened to me. Things like freezing fingers and falling into tree wells.

Those who do not venture into the splendor of Mother Nature in the winter may not know what a tree well is. Drifting snow around fir trees sometimes leaves air spaces between the tree and the snow. So when you step too close to what appears to be a tiny little fir sprouting from the snow, you fall into that void. You discover the little fir is actually eight feet tall and covered by seven feet of snow.

This is quite naturally a most unsettling discovery, especially if you make it while tip-toeing out to the bathroom in your tent booties. Even more unsettling is the discovery that one of your tent booties is still covered by seven feet of snow after you have climbed out of the tree well. As I say, I would have remembered all this if I had only kept a diary. To avoid convincing myself in the future that winter camping is fun, I started a diary on this trip. Here are some excerpts:

Saturday, 1 p.m.: I have arrived at my campsite, three miles from the trailhead. Discovered while setting up the tent that conventional tent stakes do not work in powder snow.

Saturday, 1:15 p.m.: Rigged emergency stakes with ski pole sections.

Memo to self: Remember how difficult it is to ski without poles.

Saturday, 7:30 p.m.: Eager to try my brand-new candle lantern that runs on lamp oil.

Memo to self: Remember to fill new candle lantern with oil before leaving home.

Saturday, 8:30 p.m.: Hopping back to tent in one tent bootie is difficult, as is going to the bathroom in the snow on one foot.

Memo to self: Ski pole sections make good tent stakes AND retrieve booties from tree wells. Remember to carry extra ski pole sections to hold the tent up when you use them as bootie retrievers.

Sunday, 8 a.m.: Awake to find frost covering inside of tent walls.

Memo to self: Remember not to shake tent walls free of frost from inside the tent.

Memo to self: Don't leave the water bag outside the tent in the snow.

Sunday, 8:10 a.m.: I have discovered that conventional tent stakes—while useless for holding up the tent in powder snow—make excellent tools for chipping ice from a water bag.

Sunday, 8:45 a.m.: Contact lens solution freezes at the same temperature as water. Contact lenses are extremely difficult—if not impossible—to remove intact from ice. Hot coffee will thaw them nicely, but it is important to find them before drinking the coffee.

Memo to self: If you can find your way back to the trailhead without your contacts, never go winter camping again.

THE INCOMPLEAT ANGLER

My grandfather tried to teach me how to cast a fly, but it was like trying to teach a horse to run on its hind legs.

"Tuck your elbow in," he'd say. He would stand behind my left shoulder, well out of the way of flying gray hackles. That was a good thing, because one of the only things I have ever successfully caught on a fly—to this very day—is my right ear. I caught my shoulder last fall while fishing at Cedar Lake in the Olympic Mountains and considered it a major improvement.

There is the occasional stupid trout, of course. I mean terminally stupid, so blinded by some ichthyological motive beyond human ken that it attacks my fly, floating upside-down in a pile of tangled leader and weight-forward line. For me, the best part about modern fly fishing is the trend towards barbless hooks. They are so much easier to remove from flesh, and in these days of stylish body piercing, I save large amounts of money.

Despite all this, I love the simplicity of fly fishing. It's just me, the $400 wand of carbon fiber I desecrate with every move of my casting arm, and Mother Nature. If you listen carefully, you'll hear her laughing at me above the gentle chuckle of the river.

I can hardly wait to float my new canoe, the Tipsy Tiki, on the waters of Lunker City again. That is the secret lake in the Okanogan country where I fish every spring with my friend, Grizzly Hemingway. Griz is an excellent fly fisher. He says the secret is not in casting, but in knowing how to hold your mouth. He says my grandfather taught me the proper techniques for fly casting, but never taught me to hold my mouth properly.

Last spring, the wind blew so hard at Lunker City that I could troll a fly from one end of the lake to the other without taking a paddle stroke. This entire mile-long drift took exactly two minutes and there wasn't a single trout in the lake that could keep up. Griz, lying low in the water in his spiffy float tube, just giggled when I went by so fast the fly left a rooster tail (not the tied variety). The only time he could begin to match my speed was when one of dozens of trout taking his Chironomid would drag him around the lake.

One of those trout—I'd swear to this on my grandfather's split-bamboo Peerless—was so large that Griz water-skied on his tube fins briefly until the rainbow tired. He used other anglers' float tubes as slalom markers. I have come to think that it is my duty at Lunker City to provide comic relief to all the other anglers, bored by catching and releasing two-pounders all day. Besides catching my ear, last year I fell out of the canoe and onto the shore, spraining my shoulder.

If I'd listened to Granddad, I'd have had my elbow tucked in and saved my shoulder.

PADDLING LESSONS

For reasons I am unable to explain, perfectly sane folks out there would rather paddle around in a kayak when instead they could be skiing, hiking, mountaineering, or biking. In fact, sea and whitewater kayaking are among the fastest-growing water sports.

Luckily for me, one of those perfectly sane folks is not me. I can't keep a kayak upright. I can wink at a kayak and it turns upside-down. If it is on a Thule rack, the whole car turns upside-down. Don't get me wrong: I'm a paddling expert. They wouldn't call me Mr. Outdoors if I couldn't paddle. I used to own the world's heaviest canoe, the Yellow Submarine.

I got the Yellow part from its color. I got the Submarine part because it spent as much time below the surface of Lake Slimeington as above. I would take B.B. Hardbody out onto Lake Slimeington for evening paddles. When we got far enough from shore that she couldn't swim back, I would sing romantic songs to her. Being so far from shore also kept my neighbors from hitting me with the garbage they threw at me when I started singing.

Sometimes I demonstrated my paddling expertise to B.B. Hardbody. I would demonstrate the "J" stroke and the Yellow Submarine would glide straight into a deadhead. Then I would demonstrate the common backstroke as I swam for shore. I am such an expert at paddling a canoe that I have even developed several original strokes. There is the "Z" stroke, for example. This is an excellent stroke to use if you are in no hurry to get anywhere. You simply make a Z in the water with your paddle.

But far and away the most useful stroke is the "Lazy I." You simply make a horizontal "I" in the water, perpendicular to the canoe. If you stroke towards the canoe, you capsize in the direction of the paddle. If you stroke away from the canoe, you capsize in the opposite direction. Some folks will argue that the Lazy I stroke is useless unless you like to tip over. This is patently ridiculous. The Lazy I stroke can actually be used to keep the canoe upright, as when B.B. decides she can make it to shore and dives off one side of the canoe.

I simply execute—in a manner of speaking—the Lazy I towards the canoe to counterbalance Hardbody's leap. The Lazy I is also useful when, on those rare occasions I misjudge either the distance from shore or my neighbors' throwing arms, I must move the canoe rapidly sideways through the water to avoid flying heads of rotting lettuce.

None of these strokes are useful, however, if you paddle a kayak. Since they are always tipping over on me, the only thing I know about kayaking is the Texas Roll.

This maneuver—you may call it a "womaneuver" if you wish—is executed by flailing violently and screaming loudly enough underwater that somebody could hear you all the way down in Texas. They will take pity upon you and roll you upright before you drown.

AEROBIC WARNING

Some folks have suggested that low-impact aerobic exercise is an excellent way to whip yourself into shape for outdoor activities such as hiking, mountain biking, or kayaking. I have just one question for them: **ARE YOU ALL OUT OF YOUR FREAKING MINDS?**

Aerobics can lead to big trouble in several ways.

For example, you can attend an aerobics session and get hooked. You would spend all the time you might otherwise spend getting cold and wet outside instead in some air-conditioned, comfortable gym.

Second, you might actually begin to improve your physical condition. Somebody would call you "buff," or "tough," or even "bad." You would begin to spend large amounts of paddling, riding, or hiking time rubbing your body with various oils and observing the effects in wall-sized mirrors. Clearly, there is some advantage to aerobicizing indoors on weekdays, when it is difficult to get far enough outdoors to find true misery. Still, when the urge to get down on the floor and do tummy crunches strikes, follow these instructions:

1. Run out to the garage and find your garden hose.

2. Find the muddiest part of your garden and spray it for fifteen minutes. Add at least one refrigerator tray full of ice cubes.

3. Take off your shoes and stand in the mud for thirty minutes while spraying yourself liberally with the hose.

A third danger to indoor aerobics is that you can watch them in the privacy of your own home on cable TV, and see so many hunks or babes that aerobic exercise will be the last thing on your mind. You will instead be thinking about languishing in a perfumed, foaming bubble bath while sensuous, smooth-skinned servants massage your body with hot oil.

I flipped on the TV the other day to find four babes and a hunk aerobicizing on a beach. A tropical bird counted the repetitions. My first question was: Why do the women who watch this put up with only one hunk? Why does the camera focus on the babes all the time? The bird got more air time than the hunk.

The other thing was, none of the aerobicizers was old enough to require exercise to stay in shape. When you are between the ages of eighteen and twenty-five, the only thing you have to do to say in condition is eat and drink. Any one of those babes or the hunk could have eaten the entire Sara Lee cheesecake factory and metabolized it on creating hormones alone. It seems like, if these shows are really interested in getting you to exercise, the aerobics instructors and demonstrators would be real people, not Barbie and Ken. Want me to do aerobics? Show me some ancient, balding, cranky exercisers out there, folks who can't remember the count from one move to the next.

Folks like me.

Of course, there is a certain artistry in aerobics performed by a babe or a hunk. It approaches ballet. The line. The music. The fluid movement. Crap like that.

Take my word for it, outdoors-lovers: Stay away from aerobics.

OUTDOORSPEAK

Let's talk about a vocabulary for outdoorsfolk. My friend Wimpfoot thinks that outdoorsfolk are unable to communicate with one another because they don't share any common language.

Eskimos, for example, have more than 2,016 words for "snow," each describing a different type. Outdoorsfolk should have at least as many words, he reasons, so that they can understand each other. Like, Wimpfoot coined the word *velcrud*, which is the stuff that collects in the hook side of your Velcro and makes it look all messy. He also created the word *dehydredge*, the goopy junk at the bottom of your pack that is partially reconstituted, spilled freeze-dried food.

He thought all of my suggestions were less than inspiring. I tried *taluseration*, which is a cut mountaineers get when they fall on large scree. He didn't even crack a smile at *contouropyia*, which, as all outdoorsfolk and orienteers know, is the ocular condition brought on by repeatedly trying to read lines of equal elevation on contour maps.

One word, *botulist*, sounds as if it might have something to do with food poisoning. It does not. Botulist is what happens to the bicycle whenever a bicyclist attempts to rest one side of his or her bottom. Also from the cycling world, we get the word *splotchain*. If you have ever thrown your chain, replaced it, and then wiped the sweat from your forehead, there is a good chance you got a splotchain on your forehead.

Paddlers may appreciate the word *scrigeous*. This is an onomatopoetic word that describes the sound your canoe or kayak makes when scraping across a barnacle-clad rock. It is also used to describe a paddlers' mood after her canoe scrapes across a barnacle-clad rock, to wit:

"I'm scrigeous! I left $50 worth of fiberglass on that rock."

Some other words that should be used frequently by outdoorsfolk:

—**Hiphickey**, the bruises you get on either side of your hips from wearing a heavy backpack with its hipbelt cinched too tight.

—**Forklines**, the marks left in asphalt when you forget to tighten the lugs on your front bike wheel.

—**ANSmudge**, the mark left on asphalt just beyond the forklines, made by an ANSI-approved helmet.

—**Runlikehell**, the word which should be uttered only after your hiking partner passes a yellow jacket nest on the trail and stirs them up so they rise from the nest to chase you along. Should your partner not heed your advice, you have no choice but to runlikehell up and over his or her backpack.

—**Russians**. Use this word to describe the way you feel the morning after you have consumed a whole bagful of freeze-dried Chili Taco Surprise. Use it to warn anyone within five miles that you are headed for the nearest outhouse. Scream it, in this fashion, as loudly as possible: "The Russians are coming! The Russians are coming!"

It may not be completely honest, but it certainly gets the message across.

GET IN SHAPE FOR CAMPING

Many of you will take your first camping outing of the season soon. This is an event that should not be taken lightly.

You can't just haul out the tent, cooler, stove, lantern, fishing gear, inflatable raft, portable TV/VCR combo, generator, firelogs, cookware, paper plates, water jugs, sleeping bags, air mattresses, camp furniture, and several tons of other stuff and hit the road.

No. You've got to prepare for your first camping outing of the season. Here are ten exercises that should help you get ready for camping season:

1. Set your tent up in the driveway. If you've got a camping trailer, crank up the sides and roof. Now get in the tent or trailer and ask your neighbor to turn the hose on it. Practice putting up the rain fly or zipping up the windows as you would in a real midnight rainstorm.

2. Fill your cooler with ice, hot dogs, potato salad,

mustard, pickles, and mayonnaise. Leave it outside overnight and pay Junior or Missy to scatter the contents around the yard to simulate an attack of Killer Raccoons.

3. Inflate your air mattress and place it on the coldest, hardest spot you can find around your yard. A concrete driveway, steps, or sidewalk will do nicely. Now stick a pinhole in your mattress and go to sleep.

4. Set up your new canvas folding camp chairs that came with folding drink trays and magazine racks. Hose them down real good and then sit in them for an hour. Make certain your favorite copy of *Outside* magazine gets nicely soaked before you try to read it.

5. Build a small fire in your driveway. Now dump a half-cord of green branches on top of it and inhale the smoke for thirty minutes. If you live in a no-burning area, visit the smoking section of your favorite restaurant and breathe for an hour.

6. Record your neighbor's barking dog on a 120-minute tape. Play it in the middle of the night while you are trying to sleep on your leaky air mattress.

7. Relax blindfolded in your wet canvas folding camp chairs that came with folding drink trays and magazine racks. Ask your spouse or Junior or Missy to jab at you randomly with a needle. Pretend you are swatting at stinging flies and mosquitoes.

8. Record a heavy metal or grunge band for two hours. Now play it back in the middle of the night while you are trying to sleep on your leaking air mattress. If you enjoy heavy metal or grunge, record classical music instead.

9. If you own a dog, coat it heavily with mud, sticks, leaves, and deer droppings. Let it shake itself off inside your tent or tent trailer. If you do not own a dog, let Junior or Missy try the same exercise.

10. Soak all of your camping clothes in ice water for thirty minutes. Now practice changing clothes in front of a high-speed fan.

If you live through these ten exercises, you can handle anything your first day of camping season will give you.

PRODUCT ADVISORY

We—B. B. Hardbody and I—have been tromping up and down a few local trails, trying to get into shape for hiking season. It has been especially tough on me this year, since I must take my inseparable companion, Stummick, with me wherever I go.

I am doing my best to lose Stummick; trying tricks like jogging down the trail. This has little effect because Stummick always seems to get to my destination a couple feet in front of me, no matter how fast I run. We've been picking fairly short trails and found this two-mile forest walk on the map that looked pretty easy. The map we used had no contour lines on it and we could not see that the trail climbed almost a half-mile UP into the clouds.

There was a sign at the trailhead advising hikers that anyone who could not run a mile in under five minutes should avoid the trail. But I paid no attention to that, since we all know that Forest Service and National Park officials are overly concerned these days about liability and warn hikers about things that don't really exist.

"**WARNING!**" said the sign. "**IF YOU PLAN TO HIKE THIS TRAIL WITHOUT OXYGEN, YOU MUST FIRST OFFER PROOF YOUR FINAL WILL AND TESTAMENT IS IN ORDER AT THE NEAREST RANGER STATION.**"

We started up the trail and I was delighted to find that ropes and climbing skills were not necessary for the first 100 feet. Despite his incessant growling, Stummick continued to lead me up the trail. B.B. Hardbody was wearing her best hiking boots, a pair of light mountaineering boots that won *Backpacker* magazine's highest praise a few years ago. They have served her well for several years, although she's probably put fewer than 100 miles on them. She was quite surprised, then, to find the soles of both boots were flapping quite independently of the rest of the boot by the time we reached the turnaround point.

It was as if the mid-sole of the boot had suddenly been transformed into another dimension, leaving only mud and a gaping crevasse in its place. This was not good, since we now found ourselves with two miles of trail that dropped like Yellowstone Falls to the parking area below. Hardbody might have been smarter if she had removed her boots and hiked out in her stocking feet. But the outer soles of her boots were still new, so she decided to leave the boots on for traction, even though the outer soles were clearly ready to migrate north for the summer.

By the time we reached the trailhead, she had blisters on both big toes that were easily the size of Mount St.

Helens—before it blew off its top. I would have drained them on the spot, but the resulting flood would have covered most of Nebraska and Minnesota.

If you can find them, those of you in drought areas might pick up a pair of these great boots.

MY INDOORS DOG

Tar, the Wunderhund, is an Indoors Dog. I want to make him an Outdoors Dog but he is resisting.

In the first place, he likes French food. I like French food, too, but putting sauce *Béarnaise* on Little Champions is a bit much. I took the little blighter to the vet the other day. He looked at Tar's teeth and said that if I wanted to prevent doggy gingivitis, I had better feed him dry dog food. The vet gave me an eight-ounce sample pack that cost as much as a tenderloin steak weighing the same amount.

Tar took one look at the food and asked, "You weesh for me to eat this *dechets*?"

I do not speak French, but I have learned a smattering from reading Canadian road signs and packaged food labels while mountaineering in the Canadian Rockies. Therefore I know that *dechet* is the French word for "garbage."

"It's good for you," I said.

"I weel not eat this. Bring me *haricots vert aux champignon* and *pate de foie gras*," said Tar. I took this to mean the dog wanted green beans with mushrooms and a pate of goose liver.

Some fools may complain that this conversation

never took place. They will tell you that dogs and other animals cannot talk, and accuse me of being journalistically dishonest by reporting they can. These dunces obviously have never listened to a raven croak a greeting, or a bull elk explain that it can kick the living crap out of any other bull elk within a hundred miles. All animals have developed a language at least as complex as ours and anyone who tells you otherwise has the powers of observation of a piece of granite.

Olympic National Park used to be my favorite wilderness stomping ground, but the friendly rangers in our national parks take a dim view of doggies or other pets on our trails. If your pet happens to be a llama, horse, burro, or mule, however, you can still walk most national park trails. My theory is that the larger the size of the dropping the animal leaves, the more welcome the animal is on our national park trails. Why, it is only a matter of time before the friendly park rangers allow elephants to be used as pack animals.

Thankfully, our national forest rules aren't so stupid. Forest biologists remember that pioneer trailblazers and trailbuilders had pets with them. So the Indoors Dog hikes with me in national forests. I tell each hiker we pass I'm trying to teach Tar to be an Outdoors Dog.

Many of these hikers have real dogs who are the targets of very mean insults barked at them by Tar. If any of them understood French, my poodle companion would be trail food. A sort of canine *hors d'oeuvre*. Since national forest rangers make no distinction between pack and pet animals, we also met a number of the former as well as the latter. One crusty dude rested his steed beside the trail, drinking a beer at 10 a.m.

"That there's a cute little doggie, yessir," he said. "I bet he squats to pee. Haw, haw, haw."

Tar uttered a French insult that I have never seen on a Canadian traffic sign or food label.

LETTER TO MR. GORE

There is only one way to stay dry in a rain forest: don't go into it.

One of the rainiest forests is located on Washington State's Olympic Peninsula, where it rains more than 200 inches every year. One of the wettest spots is along the Bogachiel River, where it is often impossible to tell where the river ends and the rain forest begins. Sure, some people will try to tell you they can walk six miles up the Bogachiel River trail while a hundred-year storm rages about them and remain dry. Some people insist that their waterproof-breathable raingear works so well they can carry a fifty-pound backpack all day through a rainstorm and arrive dry as a dandelion seed on the wind. These people are far too intelligent to test their raingear in such a storm. They wait, instead, for some gullible outdoor correspondent to test his raingear and report on how well it works.

It has been tested. It does not work.

Actually, the real problem is that some of it works too well. Like my Gore-Tex boots. They actually kept water out while Wimpfoot and I slogged up the Bogachiel River Trail (or was it the river itself?). The problem with the boots was that once we began wading streams, water leaked into the boots and the Gore-Tex prevented the water from wicking out. Hiking in Gore-Tex boots that are full of water is a little like lacing small lakes on your feet and striking off down the trails.

We figured we would see plenty of wildlife. Wimpfoot had his trusty camera at the ready for the many mighty elk that are known to frequent the Bogachiel River Valley. In fact, we saw one elk track, surrounded by what looked like the track made by a swim fin. It was washed away as we watched, by an unusually large tidal wave from the sky. That was it in the wildlife department.

So Wimpfoot aimed his trusty camera at wet ferns and slugs that were trying to learn to swim, and actually took a half-roll of film before the water level reached his nose. Then we swam for camp. Wimpfoot, who always gets blisters on his toes, complained on this trip that his Gore-Tex boots leaked so bad that his feet were too wrinkled to blister. I saw them. They looked like albino prunes.

Unlike my Gore-Tex boots, which worked too well, Wimpfoot's leaked like a White House gossip on CNN. But even if they hadn't, they would have filled like mine with water after the first half-mile of trail or river.

You want to stay dry in rain like this? Stay at home.

You want to hike in rain like this? Nothing on earth will keep you dry.

It became painfully clear on our hike that there would be only one way to enjoy it. Pack an umbrella, wear a swimming suit, and carry your soap-on-a-rope. Take a six-mile shower up the trail. Once you get there, you can set up your tent, take off your suit, and stand in the deluge for a minute to rinse off. Then get inside the tent, and put on all those dry warm clothes you are carrying inside a plastic bag.

You can never carry too many plastic bags on a hike in a rain forest. You need a plastic bag for your dry clothes. You need a plastic bag for your wet clothes. You need a plastic bag for your pack and two plastic bags for your booties when you have to get out of the tent in the middle of the night to go to the bathroom or to anchor the tent to a tree before it floats downriver. You need a plastic bag for the flotation device you will need to keep your head above water while you are trying to find your way back to the tent. You need a plastic bag to keep all of your plastic bags in, and you need a plastic bag to keep dry the note you have written to Mr. Gore:

Dear Mr. Gore:

How are you? I am wet.

I am sitting in the tent after walking six miles up the Bogachiel River Trail, most of which was under water. I feel certain that I can understand better what a migrating chinook salmon feels like.

Your parka worked swell for the first hour, and probably worked pretty well the second hour, too. I didn't notice, however, because I was so wet from sweat and condensation that I was unable to tell how much water was leaking in and how much was already there.

Your boots worked well, too. But I have a suggestion: Build drains in the soles so that when water leaks in over the tops of the boots, you can drain it out the bottom.

Wimpfoot isn't so happy with his Gore-Tex boots. He says his feet got wet the first time he wore them, and they wouldn't stay dry even if he hiked in the Gobi Desert.

Wimpfoot says he didn't wear his Gore-Tex parka. He wore a coated nylon parka which cost about $250 less than my Gore-Tex parka. He says that once you're wet from sweat and condensation, it doesn't matter whether your parka is breathable or not.

You know something? I think he's right.

Yours, etc.

THE RAINMAN

"Listen," I told Mother Nature, "I've paid my dues."

But Mother Nature chortled, as is her fashion, and continued to rain on my parade. While you are basking in sunshine, Mother Nature is raining on my parade.

Actually, it wasn't *my* parade. It was Steve Zugschwerdt's, a great photographer and my good friend. He shall hereinafter be referred to as The Rainman. The last time The Rainman and I went for a backpack together, it was my parade. Mother Nature not only rained, but snowed a foot and a half upon it as well—in late June.

It was The Rainman's plan to get even by holding his own parade. Mother Nature gives the rest of you less than an inch of water during June. She gave The Rainman at least that in a single day, and The Rainman conspired to see that all of it convened in my new tent. Oh, it all started innocently enough, with a 7.5-mile forced march up a rocky, dusty trail to a spot high in the

Olympic Mountains. The Rainman, whose athletic body only lacks the wings of Mercury, nonetheless moves up the trail with the speed of light.

Panting along several miles behind, I move up the trail with the speed of sweat. By the time we reach camp, my perspiration has turned the Sol Duc River to salt and migrating salmon are wondering if they actually left the ocean. So even though it does not rain the first day, my clothes are soggier than the dirty jockstrap hamper at the Seahawks training camp. While The Rainman cavorts about camp, I lie in a puddled heap, looking not unlike that slimy Olympic fungus that actually travels downhill along rotten logs.

Mother Nature began "misting" upon The Rainman's parade on the second day. It was one of those insidious mists where you don't realize you're drowning until you see the air bubbles rising past your nose. Yes, we put our expensive Gore-Tex waterproof-breathable parkas to the test. And yes, they all failed.

The Rainman brought Bob and Jim, his brothers-in-law from the dry climes, to see the Olympic Mountains in all their splendor from a ridgetop high above the Hoh River. Unfortunately, the only thing they could see from the ridgetop was the white wet cloud which surrounded them. As for the Hoh River, we would have been drier floating in it. Every now and then, The Rainman would emerge from his tent and point into the cloud—the direction didn't matter—and tell Bob and Jim, "Just over there is Cat Peak," or, "If you could see over there, you could see Mount Olympus."

Did I mention that I have a new tent? It holds water much better than it sheds it.

On the last evening of our backpack, the clouds

parted for five minutes. Bob and Jim—and The Rainman and I—gazed upon emerald peaks strung with pearly bands of snow. Pewter clouds laced with pink drifted lazily above the valley while a molten silver band marked the course of the Hoh River through the forest, far below.

It made the whole parade worthwhile.

MY SOFT HOUSES

Perhaps I've said this before, but it is so important that it begs to be repeated: A person cannot own too many tents. I myself own four tents, and despite my constant bitching, B.B. Hardbody continues to insist that her measly single tent is sufficient.

"What are you going to do when your measly single tent gets wet, or starts to smell like barf when you leave it rolled up in the closet?" I ask her.

"That's simple, dorkwad," she says. "I'll use one of yours." (Hardbody always uses terms of endearment when talking to me. Some are so dear that they cannot be printed in respectable publications.)

I just bought a new tent and it is a beauty. I got it on sale at Target. It is a big six-person tent with a full-coverage rainfly. That means that the rainfly covers the tent from the very tippy-top to the very bottomy-bottom. Unless your tent comes equipped with scuba gear, a full-coverage rainfly is essential to any tent you intend to use around the great, soggy Northwest. Hardbody's first question was, "Why do we need a six-person tent? There's only you and me and Tar, the Wunderhund."

"You can never tell when guests may drop in unexpectedly," I explain. "Besides, it's not like we have to carry this tent anywhere. It's a car-camping tent."

"That's good," she says, "because it weighs more than the car."

That's one thing I've noticed about women. They tend to exaggerate whenever they are expected to carry the object they are talking about. This is true with everything except their purses, which they insist have nothing in them, but weigh at least forty pounds.

My new tent had only one minor design flaw. It needed a window. So, I decided to sew one into the full-coverage rainfly myself. As some of you know, I have taken sewing lessons and am an accomplished seamster. Hardbody says that I can only sew so-so. I went to my favorite sewing store, Seam Ripper Sam's, and talked to Vinnie, the salesperson. I explained that I needed some vinyl for a tent window.

"What about seam-binding?" Vinnie asked. "You got to have seam-binding. And webbing reinforcement. You can't have a window without webbing reinforcement. Then there's the double-stitch nylon thread, a vinyl needle, special serger bobbins, and your basic two-headed asymmetrical stitching fribble."

I didn't think the serger bobbins were necessary, but if you can't trust your Seam Ripper Sam's salesperson, who can you trust? There was some question, too, about fitting a two-headed asymmetrical stitching fribble on my machine, which only has one head and is a single-fribble model.

The total came to $172.33, including tax. That was precisely $82.17 more than the price of the tent.

On the plus side, my new tent is the only one of its kind with a window and a semi-full-coverage rainfly.

SHORT ON WHEELS

Now—as if mountain biking weren't punishment enough—we have a new form of outdoor recreation: mountain unicycling.

For those of you who don't know what a unicycle is, imagine a bicycle with its front wheel missing. You sit on a post and pedal a single wheel, without the benefit of that life-saving thing called a granny gear.

If you are as accomplished at mountain biking as me—which is to say that my bike, the Great Emasculator, rides me as often as I ride it—you might find this new trend somewhat alarming. I mean, I can't manage two wheels without spending a good deal of time gouging ruts in the trail with my ANSI-approved helmet. Now I'm going to try it on one wheel? There will be twice as many ruts. In essence, I'll bet that mountain unicyclists have been practicing West Coast mountain biking once too often. They've been gouging their own ruts.

Here they are: a whole herd of unicyclists, starting off up this logging road. They look like a bunch of circus clowns escaped from the clownatorium. There are young ones, old folks, girls and boys, men and women. They are *racing*, if you can imagine, bouncing around in single-wheeled, single-tracked bliss like pinballs in a two-bit machine. If John Madden were describing the action, it would go something like this:

"BOINK! Did you see that, Al? That kid flew just like a drunken kingfisher. BOINK! There goes another one. WHAP! Oooh, there's a whole pile of 'em over there!"

Talk about guts. These unicyclists have got plenty of guts. Some of the guts were obvious after the spills they took. There was so much road rash going around it looked like a convention of the Society of Chronic Chicken Pox Sufferers. But in a perverse way, I admire these folks. They were out there, taking big risks and big spills, and coming up with smiles on their faces.

Every rider who was interviewed said much the same thing: they wanted to try mountain unicycling because they'd become bored with mountain biking. "All you do on a mountain bike these days," one said, "is race downhill at sixty miles an hour." If you quadrupled the maximum speed I've ever attained on the Great Emasculator, it wouldn't be six mph.

It looked like the biggest cause of spills on the unicycles were rocks and ruts in the track. The wheel stopped, but the rider kept going. It would be like hitting the front brake on your bike and doing an endo over the handlebars. Only on a unicycle, there are no handlebars. That's probably a good thing, because you can hit the ground a whole lot quicker. And since there are no handlebars, there's no place to put the brakes—which is just as well, because there are none.

I've actually considered trying mountain unicycling. I could practice by riding the Great Emasculator headlong at top speed into concrete walls. That might cool my enthusiasm, except for the fact that, as I mentioned, my top speed is about two mph.

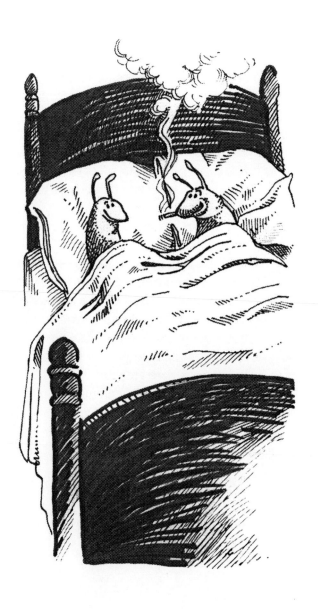

VIII.   AIN'T NATURE WONDERFUL?

SLUG SEX

PARENTAL ADVISORY: THE FOLLOWING MATERIAL CONTAINS GRAPHIC DESCRIPTIONS OF SLUG SEX.

If you or your children are offended by slug anatomy or lurid descriptions of sexual relationships between consenting adult slugs, do not read further.

You just can't go anywhere these days without running into a slug, although you can be certain that—because of the speeds they travel—a slug will not run into you. Even during dry days, you will find these gooey little gastropods trailing their slime on just about any hiking trail. Some of you don't even have to walk a trail to find a slug; if you have a garden, they will find you.

Why, down in Elma, Washington, they even celebrate the Slug Festival. You'll have to wait until July for it, though. In any event, you can see that slugs are a part of our lives as outdoorsfolk. You may be interested to know that the Northwest has one of the most dense slug populations on earth. If you don't believe me, you could ask Ann Saling, who compiled all of the following sickening facts about slugs in her 1991 book, *The Great Northwest Nature Factbook*.

This slug population boom, according to Saling, is due to the fact that the Northwest has a combination of high rainfall and soil that is low in calcium. Low calcium may also have something to do with the observation that our soil is increasingly growing in nitrogen content, thanks to the little-known fact that slug droppings are rich in nitrogen. Should the good folk of Olympic National Park ever tire of harassing wild mountain goats because they claim they are not native, they might well consider that the only native slug is *Ariolimax columbianus*, the banana slug. It is one big slimy critter, let me tell you.

Like, it grows up to ten inches long and lives for six years, assuming it doesn't drink any beer. It eats stuff like fungi and lichen and shrubbery. And—swallow your anti-emetic, parents—the spores of some mushrooms must first be passed through the digestive tract of a slug before they will germinate. Shall we talk slippery slime? Slug slime is so slippery that a slug can crawl over a razor blade without getting cut. It says so, right there on page 71.

The slug *Hemphillia* would no doubt win the Slug Olympics. It can jump two inches to get away from predators, although it is difficult to imagine anything wanting to eat a slug. Sometimes it lashes its tail, which is not half as revolting as what the slug *Prophysaon* does with its tail. A predator can grab this slippery critter, and it will detach itself from its tail. This trick is mimicked by bicyclists, who actually don't detach themselves from their tails, but certainly feel that way after riding for more than thirty minutes.

Choke on this, wildlife lovers: The black slug, *Arion*

ater rufus, rolls into a ball when it is swallowed by a bird. Then it blocks the bird's throat and suffocates it. Then it crawls out alive. But of all these sickening traits, slug sex is positively mind-boggling. **(THIS IS IT, PARENTS.)**

A banana slug mates for twelve hours, even though it is hermaphroditic. Two slugs get together, see, and circle each other while eating each other's slime trail. Maybe they are trying to figure out which is the male and which the female. Now, after they copulate **(I WARNED YOU)**, according to Saling, "one or both slugs may gnaw off the inch-long penises, perhaps because withdrawal is so difficult. The organ is believed to regenerate."

The garden slug, *Limax maximus*, is said to engage in sexual feats barely touched upon in the *Kama Sutra*. Like, two slugs climb up a tree and hang themselves on a string of slime. There they mate while "extruding a white flowerlike mass." Some of these slugs drop to the earth when spent, while others climb the slime love-string. Saling does not say whether they do any gnawing before ending their tryst.

Imagine, now, hiking along the trail. You walk under a tree and SPLAT! you feel something like a large raindrop hit your head. You reach up to feel a detumescent slug crawling around, looking for a cigarette.

Just don't say you didn't get adequate warning.

MOONING ELK

A recent power hiking trip to Banff, Alberta, left something to be desired. The scenery was spectacular, as always. The sun was bright and the sky was blue.

But when the highlight of the trip involves mooning an adult bull elk, you might guess that something in the way of excitement—not to mention good taste—is missing. Be forewarned: You are not likely to find either of those elements on these pages, either. To begin with, Wimpfoot is in love again. Wimpfoot used to fall in love about as easily as he could raise a blister on his toe, but this time it looked serious. I mean, he couldn't get through a sentence without sighing like a Chinook wind.

We departed for Canada two days behind schedule because Wimpfoot could not bring himself to leave his latest flame. It was disgusting. We drove the Coquihalla Highway from Hope to Kamloops, B.C. It is one of Canada's showcase highways, a spectacular six-lane ride through the wild mountains. It's a $10 toll to drive the highway, but they take Visa and MasterCard.

Even mine, those poor fools.

You can learn French by shopping in a Canadian grocery store, or driving on a Canadian highway. Wimpfoot was so smitten that he could not eat his *haricots vert* and sighed so long once he failed to *cedez* to a logging truck on the *Tete Jaune* highway. It was disgusting, too.

We planned a two-day hike to Berg Lake, at the foot of Mount Robson. Glaciers lick at the lake's edge while the mountain hunkers above. The *Canadian Rockies Trail Guide* said the hike was 10.8 miles, one way, and climbed 2,600 feet. All night long, I thought about climbing a half-mile and walking 10.8 miles with a 130-pound pack on my back. I know that's a heavy pack for a two-day hike. But if you know a lighter way to pack a TV, couch, generator, refrigerator, beer, and potato chips, I'd like to know about it.

When morning came, I told Wimpfoot the zipper on my sleeping bag was stuck and I couldn't get out of the bag. He sighed so hard the tent expanded like a hot air balloon. If the stakes hadn't saved us, we would have floated into the Winnebago parked next to us. As soon as I was certain it would be too late to hike to Berg Lake, I repaired the zipper on my bag. We drove to the splendid alpine country of the Icefields Parkway.

The five-mile power hike to Nigel Pass was full of killer mud. It was so slippery that the Edmonton Oilers could practice in the tundra without skates. Wimpfoot got a blister and when he sighed, he slid backward twenty feet on the killer mud.

We motored to Banff's big Tunnel Mountain Campground. In the late fall, more Rocky Mountain elk populate the campgrounds than people. Those of you who have not heard the bugling of an elk in the rut have truly missed a wilderness experience. It sounds like a squealing auto brake followed by a sound you might expect from a constipated whale: *"Wheeeeeeeeellllooooow! UGHUGHUGH!"*

It sounds very similar to one of Wimpfoot's love-sighs. Several hundred elk convened outside our tent, and every time Wimpfoot would sigh, they would bugle. Sleep was impossible. Wimpfoot complained about a sore throat and the elk bugled like an elementary school trumpet section. We were not happy campers.

When Wimpfoot walked to the phone booth around midnight to call his true love, a huge bull elk trumpeted thirty feet away. Freudians and others may explain what happened next, but I have no idea why we both turned our backsides to the elk, dropped our pants, and mooned the mighty beast.

Maybe it was the altitude or the three-liter bag of *Ch. Rotgut* (September vintage) we drank for dinner. I can only report that the elk was not impressed.

SQUIRRELING AROUND

The wildlife in Banff and Jasper National Parks is wilder than the wildlife just about anywhere. I think it has something to do with the fact that the wildlife in British Columbia and Alberta has a greater opportunity to see the Calgary Stampede than wildlife from most places.

Wildlife around my home, for example, would have to score an airline ticket to Calgary or make some kind of seriously strange migration via a ferry boat, then negotiate the Coquilhalla Highway through British Columbia. Then there would be the matter of getting into the rodeo. I mean, how would a Roosevelt elk get a ticket? It might walk up to the window and say, "What's happening, heh?"(Roosevelt elk are smart and pick up local colloquialisms, such as the Canadian "heh?".)

But Canadian wildlife has plenty of experience and has witnessed numerous rodeos and games between the Flames and Oilers. Not to mention numerous fights along the Icefields Parkway between Flames and Oilers fans.

All that is just a theory, of course.

What is indisputable fact is that a squirrel from the Olympic Peninsula has never fallen forty feet out of a tree and lived to chatter about it. Canadian squirrels apparently do it all the time. There we were: B.B. Hardbody and I settled into our car-camping tent. It once collected a goodly half of Whitefish Lake, Montana, during a July 4 rainstorm, shortly before the car blew up somewhere near Nowhere, Montana. But I digress.

So the tent was pitched in the Whistlers Campground, Jasper National Park, and a bull elk the size of Mount Rushmore wandered around outside. It wheezed and whistled like a blues singer with a serious case of the flu. Every time one of the elk cows batted its big brown eyes at one of the bachelor bulls nearby, the herd bull would stomp and mash another tree within spitting distance of the tent.

All of this was a splendid opportunity for us to observe the marvelous and mysterious ways of Mother Nature. Elk were more plentiful in the campground than campers, and they were determined to keep it that way. Yet as much noise as these monsters made, it couldn't begin to compete with the incessant chattering of a squirrel that was doing its best to tell us that the camping spot we occupied actually belonged to him. It would scold us in a voice that sounded for all the world like Howard Stern after swallowing a jackhammer.

The miniature poodle accompanying us—Tar, the Wunderhund—was only slightly bigger than the squirrel, and the two were constantly barking at one another. Between the dog, the squirrel, and the horny elk, B.B. Hardbody and I were ready for a month in a sensory deprivation tank. So I stopped to think on how I might restore peace to the campground. I couldn't kill the dog. The elk would kill me. That left the squirrel.

I walked over to the tree from which, forty feet above, the squirrel yodeled and yammered. I am not Jackie Chan. I don't even have a belt. But I whacked the tree with a mild blow with an open palm, more in good humor than anger.

Shortly thereafter, there was a furry blur before my eyes, and a considerable *SPLAT!* on the tarmac in front of me. B.B. Hardbody observed, "Good God, you've knocked that poor sucker right out of that tree."

That was impossible, I thought. Squirrels are trained from birth to hang on to limbs. How do they stay in trees during storms? But there it was, undeniably a squirrel, certainly suffering from a major case of relocation trauma. Maybe it was even dead.

The Wunderhund went over to sniff at it. Perhaps it was the elixir of a poodle's wet nose smelling at it that revived the squirrel. Who knows? Whatever it was, the squirrel leaped up and without so much as a mild squirrel curse, shot up the nearest pine like an Atlas booster in overdrive.

Squirrels, like all Canadian wildlife, can take a licking and still keep ticking. Heh?

146

IX. GOVERNMENT AND POLITICS

THE PERFECT JOB

At long last—not to mention diligent research, which entailed staring at the ceiling for at least five minutes— I've come up with a way to build my Microsoft portfolio. It involves even less work per day than that performed by your average elected official, planner, or emergency services coordinator.

This is a tough one to reveal, because I'm pretty sure there are only a few job openings in every state. Once I let the cat out of the bag, anyone who wants to get rich quick will be competing with me for the job.

There. I said it. I want to get rich quick.

I intend to become a Strategic Public Investment Tautologic Taxation Economic Reflexologist, or SPITTER. As I say, there's not a big cry for SPITTERs these days, but there soon will be. Just what might a SPITTER do, you ask? Good question, and I'll have an answer as soon as I can figure it out. I pretty much wore myself out figuring out the acronym.

OK, a SPITTER is the bureaucrat who thinks up forms of taxation that seem new, but that actually are just another way local, state, and federal governments rip people off. The tax may have a different name, like an "excise" tax, "sales" tax, "gas" tax, or "property" tax, but in the long run they all mean the same thing: You pay through the nose for something nobody is certain they really want.

Now, if a SPITTER's job stopped right there, we'd all be rushing to apply, including your average elected officials, planners, or emergency services coordinators. But there is more work to it than that. Besides thinking up a new way of prying pennies from honest peoples' hands, you've got to make them think they're getting a bargain. You've got to be willing to tell the people, "See, you'll actually save money because this new tax can only be used for building sewage treatment plants that don't smell." You must give people the impression that fewer pennies are pried from them because the money is for a sewage treatment plant that doesn't stink.

I think we can all agree that in some cases, even that ploy doesn't always work.

So the key is to create new taxes that can only be used for specific projects, then make up a whole list of projects for which those taxes can legally be used. For example, a SPITTER might suggest an entertainment tax on every household that has at least one television or radio—but the money could only be used to build public entertainment centers, such as slug-racing arenas and the like. That way, you could show the people you are prying from that they are getting a really good deal on their slug-racing arena because they are saving their property taxes for other things. Things like paying obscene amounts of money for plans that are never realized or emergencies that never emerge.

Hey: If you've lived anywhere for more than five years, I'll bet you can name one or two of those.

URBAN PLANNING

Ever since I took the introductory college class in urban planning, I have been fascinated with the notion that it is possible to plan for orderly growth. You must understand I attended college when the fastest-growing urban area was Humptulips, Washington.

That Humptulips was once the fastest-growing area in the nation is a little-known fact. Here is how it happened:

At that time, there were two people living within the greater urban area of Humptulips. Eight more settlers arrived in the spring of '09, and the community quadrupled in size in one year. Such a growth rate has not been equaled since.

The theory behind urban planning, as it was explained to me, is that you can plan for and control growth. This means the quality of your life will be greatly improved. At least, that is what my professor, Merkin Morbid, alleged. It was Prof. Morbid who started the present trend among urban planners to drive Volvos, so I am not entirely certain today that he knew what he was talking about. In any event, it is interesting to note that urban planning is still considered a valid concept. This despite the fact that no matter where you live, at least two dozen urban plans have failed within the past three days.

You need only look at the roads in front of your house to find an excellent example of urban planning in action. Undoubtedly urban planners have foreseen that your road is going to become more and more crowded with cars and little children riding bicycles, so they have improved your road with wide, paved shoulders and perhaps created passing or turning lanes so that traffic can be better accommodated. The final step is to lower the speed limit, which accomplishes two critical goals:

1. It makes driving on your road so intolerable that the crowds that moved into the neighborhood will now move out, and;

2. It increases revenue for the traffic cops who, until the speed limit was lowered, never darkened your street with their expensive laser-radar-photo speed-recording devices.

Perhaps the most visible evidence of urban planning in this state is the rapid movement of Safeway stores from one neighborhood to the next. In many cases, they move considerably faster than the traffic on your new road, and I believe—but cannot prove—that at least two Safeway stores have been cited for speeding by those same traffic cops with their expensive laser-radar-photo speed-recording devices.

See, urban planners know that as people flee from the rotting, diseased core of the city, they will not want to return to buy their groceries. So they plan for a new Safeway store about every mile or so along the new roads and they plan for a new thrift store to open up in the old abandoned Safeway store. Sequim, Washington, has the distinction of being the smallest town with the most new Safeway stores in the past two decades. The stores are moving west faster than most of the urban planners can commute from Redmond to Seattle in their Volvos.

In fact, I calculate that by the year 2008, the Sequim Safeway store, moving west along Highway 101, will pass and perhaps collide with the Port Angeles Safeway store, which is moving east. Only time will tell if I am right.

DROPPING THE SOAP

Now, let me get this straight: the City Mothers and Fathers have passed an ordinance called "SOAP." SOAP is an acronym that means "Stay Out of Areas of Prostitution."

It sounds to me like another one of those really stupid things that the City Mothers and Fathers do from time to time. In the first place, there's a big problem with the acronym. When you write an acronym, you can't just capitalize the letters you want. The rules specifically state you must capitalize all the letters. Anybody who has a problem with that can take it up with the U.S. Navy.

"Stay Out Of Areas Of Prostitution" is actually the acronym SOOAOP. Perhaps now you can see why it is a really stupid thing—SOOAOP doesn't mean anything.

I believe, but cannot say beyond a reasonable doubt, that both the state and federal governments (and perhaps some municipalities and county governments grown fat on excessive taxation and capricious grant money) employ really stupid writers whose sole job it is to make up acronyms. They pull down fat salaries like $125 grand a year to come up with phony acronyms like SOAP. I can just see them, sitting in their newly remodeled offices, brainstorming their new non-acronym:

"So, what do you think, Brian? We can call it SOAP, and everyone will think it means we plan to clean up the neighborhood."

"Brilliant, Dawn. By the way, I really like your new carpet."

The City Mothers and Fathers would identify areas of the city where prostitutes significantly outnumber Norwegian rats. Once busted in that area, prostitutes risk stiffer punishment if they return. That is the second really stupid part of SOAP, because any woman smart enough to get paid for something other women aren't is going to figure out pretty soon that she needs to move her business. And any John who is dumb enough to pay a woman for something he doesn't pay to others is going to figure out shortly thereafter that the business has moved.

So what the City Mothers and Fathers will end up with is a new area to clean with SOAP. Before you know it, the whole city will be so clean that all the prostitutes will move to another city and another source of business revenue will disappear.

Another problem with SOAP is that the neighborhood where the prostitutes work is identified. Everyone in the city now knows where to find a prostitute if they want one. Now, I did a little independent investigation in the current SOAP neighborhood and, sure enough, found a number of prostitutes. There was the prostitute pushing the baby carriage, for example, and another one coming out of the grocery store, motoring along on one of those electric wheelchairs. I saw at least two male prostitutes—one by the bank all dressed up in a fancy suit and tie, carrying an umbrella, and another with a shipyard badge going into a 7-Eleven store. It was disgusting.

Lest you accuse me of being a nattering nabob of negativism, I should point out that I have a much better solution (and, I think, a far better acronym) for handling the problem of prostitution. It is called WATER.

I wouldn't be so vulgar as to reveal what the "W" in WATER stands for. You'll just have to think of a five-letter word that is synonymous with prostitute. The other letters are short for "Attempting To Enable Relocation." See, that's a real acronym.

With WATER, the City Mothers and Fathers would name a blue-ribbon committee of prostitutes. They would meet once a month or so to discuss which neighborhoods might serve as alternate business locations and make recommendations to the City Mothers and Fathers.

Councilmen and women could then direct the prostitutes to work a certain neighborhood for the following month, then move on. Thus WATER would accomplish something SOAP will not: control the vicious spread of prostitution in our fair city. I know there are some people who will insist my plan is utterly without redeeming social value, and that is a right I would defend to the death. They must admit, however, that WATER is no phony acronym.

I'M A SEISMOGRAPH

You may find this difficult to believe, but I predicted our last earthquake. Fifteen years ago, I told B.B. Hardbody, "One of these days, we're going to have an earthquake." And sure enough, we did.

You're saying to yourself, "Big deal. Everyone knew we'd have an earthquake sometime," and you'd be correct. But how many people had the guts to say it? Listen: I predict we're going to have another earthquake. How about that? I asked Hardbody what she thought of my prediction.

"I think that perhaps you are so full of something you typically find in an unkempt horse corral that you could fertilize all of the daffodils in Skagit County," she said.

(Actually, she said nothing of the sort. I would not insult your good grace by writing what she really said.)

In fact, a number of folks are making legitimate money by predicting earthquakes in exactly the same fashion. Governments—both federal and local—pay indecent amounts of cash to really stupid people whose sole job is to tell you, "One of these days, we're going to have an earthquake."

Elsewhere, on more solid geological ground, other stupid people are being paid indecent amounts of cash to tell people, "One of these days, a volcano is going to blow up."

The prediction business isn't all fun and games, though. You could actually predict an earthquake and it would happen during your shift. That would make you responsible, and very few people want to be responsible for that kind of mayhem. Earthquake prediction is probably the easiest way to make indecent amounts of cash, though. That is because you don't have to know anything to predict an earthquake.

I was reading that the safest place to be if you are inside a building when an earthquake strikes is under a table or desk. That strikes me as an odd location: I don't own any desks or tables that can hold up my house if it decides to fall on me. Which brings me to my Get Rich Scheme of the Week. I am going to build an earthquake-proof desk. It will be constructed of pre-stressed, steel-reinforced concrete top, sides, and bottom. It will be able to withstand the weight of the average three-bedroom house. After I make my first million, I'll build an office version that can withstand the weight of the average fifty-story building.

My desks will come equipped with enough water, food, and oxygen for three days. A special executive version will have enough martinis for three days. I figure I should be able to make a bundle of dough on earthquake-proof desks for schools. Every classroom could be equipped with my desks, I told Hardbody. We'll be rich, I said.

"If they built schools strong enough to hold thirty of your desks in each classroom," she said in her best "you insipid fool" tone, "the school could withstand any earthquake."

Maybe predicting the weather would be more rewarding.

THOSE CLEVER SWEDES

Now, you've got to hand it to those Swedes, the people who bring us the only automobile you want to be inside after it crashes into a brick wall doing eighty miles per hour. They have built the *Oresundsbron*, a ten-mile bridge from Sweden to Denmark.

You might correctly point out that the Danish government shared in the $2.7 billion bridge. I have heard—but cannot verify—that their major contribution was playing Victor Borge records for the construction workers.

The bridge is really cool. From Denmark, it starts as a two-mile-long tunnel under the water. Then it traverses a 2.5-mile-long artificial island that I understand is partially constructed of Rice Krispies, which as we all know, don't get all soggy in milk or sea water. Then the bridge climbs above the waters for 1.9 miles to a high suspension span that allows ship passage. After that, it drops another 2.3 miles to Sweden, where turns into a cow path shortly after passing the first sauna.

Like most of the world's great engineering feats, the *Oresundsbron* appears to have been inspired by good beer. The Swedish word, *Oresundsbron*, after all, translates to "path over the water of the midnight sun to the land of happy suds and friendly people."

I'm certain there are some Swedes out there who will insist that *Oresundsbron* does not translate to "path over the water of the midnight sun to the land of happy suds and friendly people." But I am not talking literal translation, here; you've always got to take into account the connotations of words.

The bridge has a four-lane highway, and on the Swedish side, you'll find front, side, bottom, and top air bags. There's also a double-track railway with more crumple zones than an entire fleet of Volvos.

The bridge is expected to carry as many as 13,000 vehicles a day. The Danish figure at least 12,999 of those will be Swedes headed to Copenhagen to load up on decent beer while the one Saab weaving its way back to Sweden will have already stocked up.

"Why would we want to go over there?" one Dane asked. "Everything is expensive in Sweden, you can't drink, the Swedes are boring, and there's nothing to do."

As you might imagine, that ticked off Sven-Eric Soder of the Swedish Foreign Ministry. Sure, he said, you can get good beer, cheaper cars, clothes, shoes, food—pretty much anything you want—in Denmark. Then he pointed out that dental work is much cheaper in Sweden. You can only imagine how many Danes are going to be rushing to Swedish dentists, who, I have heard but cannot confirm, insist on using cast iron fillings covered by stainless steel, double shock absorbers, and shatterproof glass.

Now, you may be asking, "What has all this bridge nonsense got to do with me?" Nothing whatsoever.

I simply thought it was about time to provide a little evidence that at least some stupidity also exists outside our borders.

BRAINSTORMING STUPID SIGNS

After six years, I have finally figured out why I am filled with road rage every time I see a "Drive Friendly" sign.

At first, I thought it was because I get angry every time I think about the number of really stupid road signs that taxpayers are funding. Somewhere, hidden deep within the bowels of government, there is a Division of Really Stupid Signs, and it is run by really stupid people. Take, for example, the sign that sprouted like a dandelion beside one of my favorite roads the other day.

"Watch for Stopped Traffic Ahead," it says. This is an obvious example of the work of the Division of Really Stupid Signs. In fact, I'll wager that within a matter of months, there will be a rear-end collision at that sign. The driver of the vehicle that smashes into the rear of the car in front will tell the cop, "I was reading the sign and didn't see the stopped traffic ahead." Here's some advice for motorists: KEEP YOUR EYES ON THE ROAD AHEAD! DON'T READ REALLY STUPID SIGNS!

It is only a matter of time before we see some other really stupid signs beside our highways and byways. Even as you read these words, really stupid Division staffers are brainstorming:

"I got it, Dawn! A sign that reads: 'Stop for children.' "

"Great, Brian. How about one that says, 'Avoid accidents'?"

Many of the new signs will be the work of design teams. As we all know, a team is only as good as its worst player, which is the reason we have so many really stupid signs. I'll bet you've seen other examples of inane signs. How about "Drug Free Zone" signs? If you were to launch a square-mile house-to-house search around one of those signs, you would find either a meth lab, marijuana farm, bar, or tavern. I'm just waiting for someone to post a copy of that sign saying "Free Drug Zone." I'll bet nobody notices the change for weeks.

How about the "Improve Safety. Turn on Lights" sign? I'll admit, they're replacing that one with a sign that gets the real message across: "To be better seen, turn on lights."

In truth, it isn't the really stupid signs that bother me so much as the fact that government—which we all know is always begging for more money—has the funds to waste on nag signs. Instead of hiring extra law enforcement officers or traffic safety officers with the money, they instead send it to the Division of Really Stupid Signs. And that is the real reason I am filled with road rage every time I see a "Drive Friendly" sign. Nearly four decades ago, the wife of the president of the United States launched a successful campaign to rid our highways and byways of ugly, stupid signs.

Those early signs, paid for by largely private enterprise, have now been replaced by signs produced by the Division of Really Stupid Signs. You, lucky taxpayers, are paying for them.

I HAVE QUESTIONS

Maybe this happens to you, too. It happens to me all the time: Somebody says something that is really clever and all I can do is respond by mumbling something stupid.

Then, about ten days later, I think of exactly the clever thing I should have said. B.B. Hardbody says it always takes me ten days to think of something clever—and even then, it only works part of the time. For example, the great comedian Jonathan Winters once told the story of being pulled over by a traffic cop for speeding. "OK, buddy," the cop said, "where's the fire?"

And Jonathan Winters responded immediately, "In your eyes, officer."

See, that's the kind of clever thing it takes me ten days to think up. It is very frustrating because nobody cares after ten days whether you've got a clever retort or not. A traffic cop once pulled me over for speeding, years ago, and asked me where the fire was. "In my apartment, officer," I said. It was, too—so that doesn't count as a clever retort.

Another thing that happens to me a lot is that I think of questions I would ask people if it were any of my business. I never ask the questions, though, because it isn't any of my business. For example, if it were my business, I would ask a bunch of questions about the recently completed three-year government program of monitoring water around my neck of the woods. The first question I would ask is: How much did it cost?

The second question I would ask is: Why did it take

you guys so long? All you really have to do is look at the icky, gooey, slimy things in the water to tell if it is polluted. Like, I live on Lake Slimeington, the third-most-polluted lake in my neck of the woods. Believe me, you don't have to study Lake Slimeington for three years to figure it is polluted—all you have to do is put your foot in it and when your toenails start to shrivel, you know the lake is polluted. Lake Slimeington is so polluted that all of the bass in the lake are pickled. Ducks that swim in the water are bald from their waterlines down. It's enough to make a birdwatcher bawl.

Another question I would ask is: How can the area's sixth-cleanest stream flow into and out of Lake Slimeington, the third-most-polluted lake? Maybe that is what took the government three years to figure out.

One of the reasons we have all this dirty water, we are told, is because a whole bunch of septic tanks are failing. That took long and expensive study—when all you really have to do is walk around your neighborhood and see whose turf is looking really good without fertilizer.

Which brings up another question I would ask if it were any of my business. I would ask this: Weren't all of those septic tanks that are failing tested and approved by the local government? Doesn't the local government see designs and tests of every single septic tank in the area before it is installed?

If I were in charge of testing and approving all the septic tanks installed in this county in the past twenty years, I'd be a mite concerned. I'd hop in my Volvo and take a long holiday to Brazil.

I suppose a whole bunch of people have very clever

and immediate answers to all these questions. But I know it would take me at least ten days to answer any single one.

I'M A DUNDERHEAD AND PROUD OF IT

I got my Official Voter's Pamphlet the other day. It was a great relief to me to learn that there are so many candidates of such high caliber seeking to serve us.

In fact, I was inspired by the statements of all of the candidates who want to serve us. So inspired was I that I have decided to form my own political party and run for something next year. It has to be a new political party, so that it won't suffer from the stereotypes we have of our present political parties. I will name my new party the Dunderhead Party. The Dunderheads will defy stereotyping.

You know the kind of stereotypes I am talking about. Stereotypes like:

"All Republicans are wealthy and represent the interests of business over the interests of human beings."

And:

"All Democrats are poor and represent the interests of human beings over the interests of business."

We all know those stereotypes aren't true. I'll bet you can show me a dirt-poor Republican who represents human beings over business. And I'm certain I can show you a rich Democrat who represents business instead of human beings.

But Dunderheads won't represent anyone but themselves. The Dunderhead Party will bring a new element to the American political process. The element will be called "honesty." I haven't figured out exactly what position I'll file for yet, but it won't matter. My Official Voter's Pamphlet statement will be the same:

I have lived in this community longer than dirt. I have no intention of doing anything for you. My purpose in running for this noble office is to draw a big fat salary for essentially doing nothing for the next four years.

You should vote for me because I am a Dunderhead. If I am elected, you can be certain that I will represent nobody but myself.

That may seem like no big deal to you, Bucko, but just think about this: Let's say you vote for that Republican candidate, and the Democrat wins. You are not only un-represented, but that no-good Democrat is going to do everything he or she can to see you don't get squat for the next four years.

But if you elect a Dunderhead like me, there is a slight possibility that some of your interests may coincide with mine. Just think about that before you pull that party-line handle.

Another thing: You can never be certain that stupid Democrat or Republican believes in the same things you believe in. But I'm a Dunderhead—I'll believe in anything you want, just so long as you vote for me.

In closing, I'd just like to say there's nobody who likes apple pie more than me, that I'll take a Ford over a Chevy any day of the week (as long as it doesn't have Firestone tires on it), and that my mother was the best female parent I ever had.

If you're interested in sending a campaign contribution, mail it to The Dunderhead. Be aware that I take cash in $300 bills only.

BUMMERVILLE

I am a nut for computer games. They are cool. I have one.

I used to have many computer games. I had a flight trainer and I got to fly my virtual single-engine Piper Cub into tall buildings in virtual Chicago. And I had a game that let you create your own virtual city, then run it like you would a real city. I named my city Bummerville, because I was very depressed on the day I got my virtual city game. I played with Bummerville for about three days straight, but accidentally let the sewage treatment plant overflow on the fourth day. Bells and whistles went off, a siren screamed, and a big mushroom cloud flashed on my computer screen with two words in neon green:

"Game Over."

Shortly after that, I got my new iMac. It is a splendid computer for a dewhead like me, or anyone who wants to use a computer without suffering through fifteen years of classes on how to run DOS. The biggest problem with my iMac is that it doesn't like to play games. I was able to solve this problem with something called Virtual PC, which allows my iMac to run Windows software. Computer owners know what I am talking about and I would ask the rest of you to laugh aloud at this point so that people will think you are reading something funny.

Anyway, the first thing I did was rush out and buy a new copy of Bummerville. It has some new features and I told B.B. Hardbody I just had to try them out. She thought the program cost too much.

"C'mon," I said, "it's just software."

"You're SO full of software," she said. She cackled at her little joke like a cricket on a heavy metal amplifier.

One of the features on my new Bummerville game is an urban planning feature. You can manipulate the urban plan so that your virtual city grows wherever you want it. Like, you can say your city is going to grow by 20,000 people over the next twenty years. The game allows you to do that, even though your virtual city's population has actually shrunk in the last twenty years.

And you can plunk a virtual development down on almost any worthless piece of virtual forest or wetland. You can tell the computer that your virtual development will have 1,200 homes and that 2,000 people will live in them. The computer will not question the fact that is only 1.6 persons per household, because this is only a make-believe city.

The best part about Bummerville is that the sewage treatment plant can overflow every day, but you can keep playing the game. You can wreak all sorts of virtual havoc with your virtual city without crashing your computer.

My Bummerville now has fifteen urban centers, all served by their own highway, sewer, and transportation systems and really stupid planners and emergency coordinators. It gets a little confusing when you are trying to find City Center, but it is only a game.

X. I GET LETTERS

MY VIEW OF YOUR VIEWS

One thing I always read in my favorite daily newspaper is the "YOURVIEWS" section on the Opinion Page. Some newspapers call it "Letters to the Editor"—which seems to me to be more precise—but it does take up more space.

YOURVIEWS is always interesting because it enables me to take the pulse of our community. It shows me how people think about the issues of vital importance that affect our daily lives. I am especially encouraged by the overwhelming number of letters that are written about overpopulation, conservation, global warming, the extinction of species, the growing oil crisis, and racism. A letter addresses one of those subjects at least once a quarter.

Some people write letters to me. Most letters, I'll admit, are not too complimentary—but every now and then, somebody writes something that warms the very cockles of my soul.

For example, a guy once called me a "hack Dave Barry Wannabe." I consider being put in the same sentence with Dave Barry—even as a hack wannabe—the highest compliment.

Then, the other day, another guy wondered why my favorite newspaper would publish my "demented, bigoted ravings." I've often wondered that, myself, but I was hoping nobody else would notice. This same gentleman suggested that I could kiss his ___, which brings me more or less to my topic. Generally speaking, the act of kissing is regarded far and wide as a sign of love and respect—except if you are asked to kiss someone's ___.

For example, if the letter had said, "Seabury Blair can kiss my lips," I would consider it a high compliment, except for the fact that the letter writer is a man and I am not gay (sometimes not even happy). And if he had said, "Seabury Blair can kiss my cheek," I might conclude the writer is French and offering a common greeting. I also like the double entendre on that one.

But beyond that, I am a little disappointed that such a mild vulgarism as ___ would be censored. After all, the very act of removing the word that describes that fleshy, bulbous part of the human anatomy directly below and on either side of the spine from YOURVIEWS makes the word seem even more vulgar.

Further, the letter writer may have been instructing me not to kiss his ___, but to kiss his donkey instead. As I am certain most of you know, when you refer to a donkey in the newspaper, it is perfectly acceptable to write "ass."

You can also probably refer to a fool or blockhead as an "ass" and get away with it in a newspaper. But if you are asking someone to kiss your ___, you'd better come up with another word for it or everyone is going to wonder what you meant.

The big problem with censoring the word, it seems to me, is that you're going to have to be consistent. Thus, when the sports guys (the Sports Page is another of my most favorite parts of the paper, because sports and police writers are the only true reporters left on daily newspapers) are told by the coach, "He fell on his ___," they won't be able to print it. If, on the other hand, a Western guide trips over his pack animal, there would be no problem with writing, "He fell on his ass."

Similarly, if your boss is quoted in the newspaper as saying, "I wish she'd get off her dead ___," it would not be printed. But if you were riding a donkey up a Grand Canyon trail, and it had a heart attack, there would be no question about quoting the ranger in the paper as saying: "I wish she'd get off her dead ass."

Anyway, keep those cards and letters coming. They are the backbone of the paper, so to speak.

FAN MAIL

The old e-mail bag has been buzzingly full lately. My e-mail provider is Dreary Rude Oldies On Line, DROOL—and they only let me keep twenty-five electronic epistles on file before they start charging mailbox rent.

So I thought I'd answer a few letters right here, right now:

Dear Hack Dave Barry Wannabe:
I tried your recipe for Frito Pie last week and thought

it sucked. If you are going to give out recipes, why don't you give out recipes that taste good?

If you print my name, I'll leave my next Frito Pie on your car seat.

—Name Withheld by Request

Dear Withheld:

It is very difficult to go wrong with Frito Pie. After all, it is just canned chili, Fritos, grated cheese, sour cream, jalapenos, and onions (optional). Perhaps you forgot to open the can.

It is also possible that you don't like chili. It gives some people enough gas to power an Atlas booster. Try the following recipe and see if you don't like it better:

LOBSTER HUMIDOR

1 medium lobster tail per person
1 medium Havana cigar (accept no substitute!)
1/2 pound butter, melted
lemon wedges

Broil lobster tail, dip in melted butter, and eat. Smoke cigar afterward or, better still, give it to an enemy and tell them to inhale.

Yours,

—Wannabe

Dear Hack:

A while back, you wrote that there is an Assistant Director of Paint-Striping and Reflector-Gluing in the Washington Department of Transportation, and that the position paid an annual salary of $155,000.

I wish to advise you that you are in error and to demand a correction. The position pays a salary of $154,000.

Indignantly Yours,

Brian Ripoff, Director, Paint-Striping and Reflector-Gluing, Washington Department of Transportation

Dear Brian:

I apologize. I was adding the annual $1,000 incentive pay you give to any staffer who can write meaningless office memos over 10,000 words.

Sincerely,

—Hack

Dear Wannabe:

How come you are always making fun of Volvos? Crash tests prove they are one of the safest cars on the road.

Maybe you should do a little more research before you go and write all your stupid stuff.

In haste,

A. Planner

Dear A.:

You are absolutely correct. I was going to research the Volvo that passed me at the top of Snowy Pass last Saturday, going about seventy-five miles per hour.

Unfortunately, by the time it got to the top of the pass, it had done a 360-degree spin, caused another vehicle to spin, slammed into a snowbank, and pretty much obliterated everything but its thirty-two air bags. You can bet that most of the traffic that was waiting to clear the wreckage was relieved to know the really stupid driver was in such a safe car.

Yours,

—**Wannabe**

MY FIRST LOVE

In spring, they say, a young man's fancy turns to thoughts of love. Now I have discovered an old man's fancy turns to trying to remember thoughts of love.

Another thing about old men: It is easier to remember thoughts of love long past than it is recent thoughts of love. Thus it is that I remember vividly my first love, back in fifth grade. Her name was Jill and that was about all I knew about her except that my good friend Bill had heard from a friend of his that Jill had told a friend of hers that she liked me. When your love life is constructed of information that is filtered through so many sources, you deserve someone about whom you know nothing.

Actually, I learned a lot about Jill in a very short time. Her father had a sailboat and made karmel korn. She could hit a softball farther than any boy in fifth, sixth, or seventh grade. On our first date, we chopped down a big pine tree. That was my idea, but as you might guess, she did most of the chopping because I simply couldn't swing the ax half as hard as Jill.

We chopped the tree down because I wanted to get a look at the woodpecker's nest at the top of the tree. Jill was the only one who could climb the tree, but refused on the silly premise that she was wearing a dress. I told her the dress never stopped her from whacking a baseball farther than anyone in school or beating up Pat Pugh when he swiped her Big Hunk. She said that was different; somebody messing with your candy bar was serious stuff.

I planned the cutting so the tree would fall just so, between two saplings to the south. I showed Jill where to cut and chips began flying like horse flies around the barn. She made the undercut in about three mighty whacks and then moved over to the other side of the tree. She swung that ax harder than her Louisville Slugger and in very little time, that pine began to sway.

As luck would have it, it swayed quite the opposite direction from my careful plan, and toppled with a resounding thud to the north. This actually turned out to be fortunate on two counts:

1. We were standing on the south side of the tree when it fell, and:

2. If it had fallen south, we would have discovered that the woodpecker's nest was now about two feet under the springtime mud. Not even Jill's Herculean arms could have lifted that tree. Fortune was also with the woodpecker. The bird that had put the hole in the tree no longer lived there and the nest had been abandoned years before.

Jill dumped me and took up with my friend Bill shortly thereafter. I think she did so simply because she liked the sound of Jill and Bill, Bill and Jill.

It's funny. The name of my second love escapes me.

FAN MAIL II

It's time to hear from one of my former readers:

I found it very disturbing to read your article this morning. Although I am not a tree-hugger, I do love them and find it reprehensible that you found it necessary, even as a young boy, to end a lovely Pine tree's life and for the express purpose of checking out the living quarters of a Woodpecker (which I find equally distasteful).

I was born and raised in this state and in my youth, we used to climb to the tops of tall Firs, but never did we entertain the idea of cutting them down. Too much of that is currently being done.

I sincerely hope that your column is not read by impressionable youths who think that's a cool thing to do.

—**Nature Lover**

Thanks for the reality check, Nature Lover. You are absolutely right.

It was a reprehensible act and I apologize to you and the tree, which was quite dead before we whacked it down. My girlfriend, Jill, did most of the work and if I ever see her, I'll pass your admonition along.

I have made two assumptions about your letter:

1. I assume that by writing "Although I am not a tree-hugger, I do love them . . ." that you love trees, not tree-huggers. Of course, it is perfectly OK to love tree-huggers, too.

2. When you wrote you thought "checking out the living quarters of a Woodpecker" was distasteful,

I assume you meant the act of checking out was distasteful, not the woodpecker. I have never eaten woodpecker.

OK, OK, there was that time back in 1976 when I would gladly have eaten the woodpecker that Swiss-cheesed my house. But it was either $1,600 worth of cedar siding or the bird. (Lest another Nature Lover take offense, I should add that the house-eating woodpecker moved into a tree next door that I did NOT chop down. We lived in harmony until the neighbor's cat got lucky one day.)

I, too, am greatly concerned that impressionable youths may think it is cool to cut down trees. I worry sometimes in this day and age of banning books that most impressionable youths don't have the opportunity to—or more worrisome still, cannot—read, but that is another subject.

So, if any of you impressionable youths are reading this, let me say quite emphatically:

DO NOT CHOP DOWN TREES!
IT IS NOT COOL!

If your dad or mom gives you a chainsaw for graduation, I urge you to take it back and trade it in for something that cannot be used to cut down trees. Trade it in for something more environmentally sensitive, like a jet ski or snowmobile.

To be quite honest, though, I am grateful to certain tree-choppers. These people make the paper upon which is printed such worthy tomes as *Should Trees Have Legal Standing?* by Christopher D. Stone; or for a far lesser worth, these very words.

You may rest assured, however, that my tree-whacking days are over. Green on, Nature Lover.

Printed in the United States
40188LVS00001B/79